HOUSE PLANT
MADE EASY

JEAN TAYLOR

Illustrated by
Tony Streek

TVTimes
FAMILY BOOKS

INDEPENDENT TELEVISION BOOKS LIMITED, LONDON

INDEPENDENT TELEVISION BOOKS LTD.
247 Tottenham Court Road,
London W1P 0AU

© Jean Taylor 1975

ISBN 0 900 72733 0

Printed in Great Britain by
Butler & Tanner Ltd.,
Frome and London.

ACKNOWLEDGMENTS
The publishers would like to thank the following for permission to reproduce the photographs in Part 2:

A-Z, pages 76a (below), 86b, 93b; *Barnaby's Picture Library* and *Bernard Alfieri*, pages 67b, 70a & b, 71b, 76a (top), 79a, 81a & b, 85b, 87b, 94b, 96a; *Rochford's House Plants*, pages 65a & b, 66a & b, 67a, 68a & c, 69a, 72b, 74a, 75b, 76b, 77a, 78a & b, 79b, 80b, 82b, 84b, 85a, 85 (inset), 86a, 88a & inset, 89a & b, 91a (top) & b, 92b, 96b (above); *Harry Smith Collection*, pages 66b, 70 (inset), 73a & b, 74b, 81 (inset), 92a, 96 (centre); *Peter Hunt*, pages 68b, 69 (inset), 90a, 94a; *Sutton & Sons Ltd.*, pages 72a, 83a, 84a, 87a, 91a (bottom), 95b.

Cover photographs taken by *Peter Smith* with the co-operation of *Rochford's House Plants*.

CONTENTS

INTRODUCTION

House plants are now a part of our way of living and are to be seen in most homes and many offices. Not only are they enjoyable in themselves, but they are attractive and decorative, relieving the bareness of rooms in the same way as paintings and ornaments.

Many people gain immense satisfaction from growing and caring for plants especially in the immediate environment of their home. For people without gardens they provide a necessary contact with nature which gives infinite pleasure. Most house plants are easy to look after, are never out of season and thrive in conditions that are suitable for their individual requirements.

The first part of the book explains the general needs of plants and describes how to look after them, including advice on watering, feeding, repotting and propagation. Plants for specific conditions are listed so that the correct variety may be selected for warm or cold rooms, light or dark places, dry or moist air and so on. The art of display is discussed in sections on featuring plants, and on making troughs, bowls, *pot-et-fleur* and bottle gardens.

The second part of the book contains photographs of easy-to-grow and popular house plants which are readily available. Underneath each photograph, which provides quick identification, instructions about the care of the plant illustrated are given in note form for easy reference.

THE MEANING OF WORDS

Acaricide: A chemical spray or dust used for destroying spider mites

Aerial root: A root arising on stems above ground as found on *Monstera*

Aerole: A pincushion-like modification on many cacti usually with woolly or barbed hairs and spines

Air-layering: A method of propagation in which a shoot is made to form roots in the air, and not in soil, while still attached to the parent plant

Annual: A plant that completes its life cycle from seed to seed in one growing season

Axil; axillary: The angle between a leaf and stem from which further growths arise

Bottom-heat: Heat applied from below as in an electric propagator for seeds and cuttings

Bracts: Modified leaf-like structures sometimes highly coloured as in poinsettia and shrimp plant

Break: To grow out from an axillary bud. This happens when the growing tip of a stem is removed and it results in a bushier plant

Bud: A swelling containing immature leaves or flowers tightly condensed which, given the right conditions, begins to grow

Bulb: A storage organ like a bud in shape usually underground, which contains the young plant

Bulbil: A small immature bulb often seen at the base of mature bulbs

Cactus: A succulent plant belonging to the *Cactaceae* family and originating in arid conditions

Cambium: The growing tissue just beneath the bark of woody stems

Compost: A composition or compound used for growing plants in pots; usually a mixture of loam, peat, sand and other ingredients. This term also refers to plant remains stacked together which, when decayed, form a humus to return to the garden. Soilless compost does not contain loam

Corm: A plant storage organ with a thickened stem base and a papery skin

Crocks: Broken pieces of clay pot which, when placed concave side down over the hole in a flower pot, provide good drainage and prevent water from collecting at the bottom of the pot as this is bad for the roots of plants

Crown: Generally used to describe the upper part of a rootstock from which shoots grow

Cutting: A leaf, bud, section of leaf, root or stem which is removed from a living plant. Under certain conditions it can become a new plant

Damping off: A diseased condition of seedlings caused by certain fungi creating rot near the soil level — encouraged by excessive humidity, poor drainage, unsterilized soil and overcrowding

Division: Pulling or teasing roots apart to make more than one plant

Dormant: Resting, with house plants this is normally in the autumn and winter, when the plant makes little new growth

Drawn: A term applied to plants that have become unusually tall, thin and pale, usually through lack of light

Drill: A straight, shallow furrow for sowing seeds

Feature plant: A specimen plant which is normally large and can be viewed from all angles as a special decoration

Fertilizer: Plant food. Inorganic fertilizers are of mineral origin either natural or manufactured. Organic fertilizers are derived from animal matter (such as bone meal) or dead plant remains. For house plants inorganic substances and concentrated organic ones are available in liquid form. They are quick acting and supply plants with essential nutrients, including nitrogen which promotes leaf and stem growth, potash for good flowers and phosphates for strong roots

Forcing: Treating plants to make them flower before the natural time

Fungicide: A substance used for getting rid of fungus diseases

Germination: The earliest stage in the development of a seed

Habitat: The natural abode of a plant, its original place of growth

Hardening off: Gradual acclimatization to cooler conditions

Heel: A small piece of old wood or stem that is deliberately pulled away when taking a cutting. Some cuttings root more easily if they have a heel

Humus: The residue when dead vegetable matter finally breaks down

Insecticide: A substance used for killing insects; may be a liquid or a powder

John Innes compost: Not a trade name, but a standardized formula for a mixture of sterilized loam, peat, sand and other ingredients. Normally seed compost for seeds, No. 1 for very small pots, No. 2 for pots from 3 to 4½ inches, No. 3 for pots of 5 inches and upwards

Joint: The points on a plant stem at which leaves or leaf buds appear

Layering: A method of propagation in which a shoot is made to form roots in soil when still attached to the parent plant

Leaf-mould: Partially decayed dead leaves which look brown and flaky. Sometimes used in compost

Loam: Garden soil

Midrib: The large central vein of a leaf

Node: A stem joint, in some cases slightly swollen. Leaves, buds and side shoots arise from it

Offset: A young plant that arises naturally, close to the parent plant

Peat: Organic matter partially decayed and usually derived from sphagnum moss. It breaks down soil giving it a good texture. It contains little food for plants

Pinching: Removing the growing point of a stem, usually to promote branching and bushiness. It can be done with the finger and thumb or with a knife. This may also be called 'stopping'

Plunge: To set a pot in a special bed of ashes, peat or sand to prevent rapid drying out and to keep cool

Potting: Placing a plant and compost in the container in which it is to grow

Potting on: Removing a plant from a container and planting it in a bigger one

Pricking off/out: The first planting out of seedlings, when they are separated

Propagation: The increase of plants by such methods as division, cutting, sowing seeds

Pruning: Controlled cutting back of a plant to restrict size or to train or shape

Relative humidity: The percentage of moisture in the air in relation to full saturation

Resting: The period when a plant makes no extension growth

Rib: One of the main prominent veins of a leaf

Runner: A type of aerial stem which on contact with soil sends down roots and begins to form a new plant

Seedling: A young plant with a single stem – immediately after germination

Seedpan: Any container in which seeds are sown

Spathe: A sheath surrounding a flower. It often looks flower-like

Sphagnum moss: Bog moss with water-retaining properties, the main ingredient of peat. It also cleanses and aerates

Staking: Supporting plants with a cane or stake

Stopping: See *pinching*

Striking: Preparing a piece of a plant to encourage it to root. A struck cutting has grown roots

Succulent: Any plant with thick, fleshy leaves or stems adapted for living in a dry atmosphere

Tamp: To firm down soil lightly

Tissue: The structural materials of a plant

Tender: The term applied to any plant that can be damaged by frost or cold

Top dressing: A layer of soil replacing one or two inches of old soil on top of the pot

Transpiration: Continual natural water loss from leaf, stem and flower surfaces

Transplant: To remove and replant a plant

Tuber: A thickened fleshy root which is a storage organ during the resting season

Tubercule: A small knob-like prominence on a plant

Umbel: A flowerhead in which the individual flower stems arise from a common point, as in an umbrella

Variegated: Shows more than one colour; usually pertains to leaves

METRIC CONVERSION TABLE

More and more terms are being metricated, so here is a rough short metrication table to help you with your indoor gardening

Inches	Centimetres	Feet	Centimetres
1	2·5	1	30
2	5	2	61
3	8	3	91
4	10		
5	13	Feet	Metres
6	15	4	1·2
7	18	5	1·5
8	20		
9	23		
10	25		
11	28		
12	30		

PART ONE—
CARE AND DISPLAY

BRIEF HINTS FOR GROWING HOUSE PLANTS

Plants must have light in order to grow and should be placed near windows.
Summer sunshine is much too hot for most of them.
Excessive heat is bad for plants.
Draughts are bad but fresh air is good.
Plants should always be in frost-free rooms.
In cold weather do not leave plants near a window and behind a curtain.
Plants grouped together usually grow better.

Most plants need spraying with water every week.
Spraying is essential in dry rooms.
When watering, water well and on to the compost.
Do not give daily dribbles of water.
Never water wet compost.
Tepid water is better than cold water.
Water less often in winter.

Buy a good plant to begin with.
Use compost sold in bags for house plants.
Plant in pots only a little bigger than the root ball.
Feed with liquid fertilizer for house plants from March to October, following instructions.
Do not feed during November to February when plants rest.
Do not use aerosol sprays near plants.

CHOOSING A PLANT FOR THE HOME OR OFFICE
WHERE TO BUY

A healthy indoor plant is usually the result of careful choice at the time of buying. A reputable shop or garden centre where plants are well cared for is the best source of supplies: if a plant is left outside on the pavement in all weathers it will probably suffer damage which may not be noticeable until well after it is taken home. It is better therefore to buy from someone who knows something about plants and takes care of them.

MAKING A CHOICE— POINTS TO CONSIDER

SITUATION
Whenever possible decide where the plant will stand before buying; whether that position is sunny, light, shady or dark; and whether the air around it will be hot, warm, cool, cold, fluctuating, damp or dry. These factors should determine the type of plant you buy, for there are house plants to suit a variety of lighting, thermostatic and atmospheric conditions. A plant growing in conditions it likes will thrive and give no trouble.

SIZE
Consider the space that will be available for the plant and choose one that will seem in proportion to its surroundings. For example, you would need: a small one for an office desk, so that it will not get in the way; a large feature plant for the bare corner of a room; a trailing plant for hanging up; a tall thin plant for a narrow windowsill.
The retailer should be able to advise on the eventual size of the plant and its speed of growth.
It is advisable to buy the biggest plant of its kind that is available and that you can afford, as there is nothing like a good start and many plants grow very slowly.

COLOUR
The majority of house plants grown for their foliage are green. However there are a number with very lovely leaves in brown, red, grey, purple, yellow and many that are variegated.
Green seems to harmonize with any colour scheme in a room. Other colours should be considered in relation to the overall effect when seen next to other furnishings such as curtains, wallpaper and cushions, as the plants are after all a part of the decoration of the room. For example a bright yellow chrysanthemum plant could be too strong in colour for a room decorated in subtle pink.

FLOWERING PLANTS

A plant full of flowers and buds is very tempting but is rarely in bloom for long and once the flowers fade it can look quite dismal. If a plant with a long, attractive life is wanted it is wiser to choose a plant grown for its foliage rather than its flowers. If you are prepared to enjoy a flowering plant for only a limited time then one with many buds and only a few open flowers is a better buy—it will last longer than one in full bloom which could be near the end of its flowering time.

GROWING REQUIREMENTS

Many plants now carry a label stating whether or not they are easy to grow and brief advice on how they should be treated for the best results. Unless you are experienced, it is more practical to buy a plant labelled 'easy'; those marked 'delicate' or 'intermediate' may be tricky to keep alive unless exact conditions can be fulfilled. Some plants for example need an even high temperature or constant spraying with water. However attractive and tempting they may be, it is better to resist buying them as they may give pleasure for only a short time. There are many plants to choose from that are not demanding and will suit a variety of conditions. A healthy, hardy, actively growing plant is very much more attractive to look at than a delicate specimen struggling for life.

All the plants illustrated in this book should be easy to grow.

WHAT TO LOOK OUT FOR

Buy a plant that looks healthy and clean. If possible it should show some fresh new leaves or shoots.

A bushy plant of pleasing shape is more attractive than a leggy one, which is unlikely to improve with time.

The soil in the pot should be moist, as very dry or soaking wet soil may be indicative of careless treatment in the shop.

There should be no obviously missing leaves or any that are damaged or yellowing, as these too are signs of ill-treatment.

TAKING THE PLANT HOME

The plant should be wrapped for protection especially in winter. It will have been grown in a warm greenhouse, packed in a special box and displayed in a sheltered shop. If it is suddenly exposed to cold air, wind or draughts it will probably suffer permanent damage.

A plant takes a little time to become acclimatized to a new home and needs gentle treatment for a week or two. Place it in the chosen position (provided this is away from draughts and direct sunlight) and give it water only if it seems very dry (with the exception of *Azalea indica* and *Hydrangea* which die if they are allowed to dry out).

NECESSARY EQUIPMENT

When buying the first house plant little equipment is necessary.

WATERING CAN

A can that holds not less than one pint and has a long narrow spout for directing the water exactly into the pot is the most useful. Small cans, which need filling often, discourage sufficient watering. The long narrow spout can be placed close to the soil to avoid splashing water on to the furniture.

SPRAYER/ATOMIZER

Special ones are made for the purpose of spraying leaves of house plants with a fine spray. One holding about a pint of water is useful.

PLANT SAUCER OR OUTER POT

It is better to leave the plant in the pot in which it was bought, at least for a while. In time it may need transferring to a bigger pot but it is better to purchase this when required.

All plant pots have drainage holes in the bottom, which means that water will leak on to the furniture and make a mess. (If a pot does *not* leak, it is unlikely that the plant is receiving enough water!) To avoid marking furniture it is better to place the pot in a plant saucer. These are cheap and easily available. Alternatively, a decorative outer pot, which does not have holes in the bottom, can be used. There are many of these available in all sizes, colours and textures, both antique and modern, and expensive or inexpensive. The outer pot or saucer should be about 2 inches bigger in diameter than the inner pot so that there is about 1 inch of air space all around between the two pots.

PEBBLES

It is a good idea to place half an inch of pebbles in the decorative pot underneath the plant pot. Water then drains into the pebbles which stop the plant from sitting in water and getting its roots waterlogged.

FOOD

A bottle of liquid fertilizer, especially made for house plants, will be needed sooner or later.

SPONGE

Plants with smooth foliage need cleaning sometimes and a small sponge is ideal for this job.

THERMOMETER

A room thermometer is helpful to give the temperature in various parts of a room; this eliminates a lot of guesswork.

HOME AND OFFICE CONDITIONS

How easy it would be if all plants could grow well in any position—sunny windows, dark corners, cold rooms and so on—but plants vary in their requirements. This applies equally to those that are easy to grow and to the more difficult ones. However this is what makes growing them rather a challenge and makes each variety interesting and individual.

There are certain ideal conditions for each variety of plant although many grow reasonably well in other places that are not ideal. It is not always possible to find just the right place, but normally a satisfactory position is available.

Plants need: light in varying strengths; air which is suitably warm or cool; water in differing amounts; a damp or dry atmosphere; food at certain times.

Food and water are easier to provide and regulate than the other requirements: the amount of light, the temperature of the air and the relative humidity (damp or dry atmosphere) are governed by the room in which the plant is placed and are not easily altered. These conditions are normally made to suit the people who occupy the rooms and not the plants. The plants' comfort is secondary and few of us are, for example, prepared to live in a damp atmosphere so that our plants will thrive.

Consequently it is half the battle to decide where the plant is to live permanently and to buy one to suit these conditions.

Sometimes a house plant is a gift and, although warmly received, it may be difficult to place it in suitable conditions. The only solution is to place it in a position that most closely approximates to the ideal.

LIGHT

This is much more important than many people realize.

Most plants need a great deal of light and indoors there is very much less light available than out of doors. The bigger windows of modern houses and offices let in much more light than the windows of traditional homes and have made growing house plants very much easier.

The available light may be: sunny most of the day; sunny some of the day; light but without direct sunshine; shady; dark; artificial light.

No plants can live in continual darkness and only a few can stand direct summer sun and deep shade. Some will grow well under artificial lights, but the majority grow better in good natural light and as a general rule

it is best to place plants in the lightest possible position available in a room. This is normally near a window but out of direct summer sun (i.e. away from south- and west-facing windows). Winter sun is weaker and less damaging.

WINDOWSILLS

Windowsills are an obvious place to put plants. In parts of Europe they are built with special facilities and plants can be seen in nearly every window of houses and offices. When constructing a new house or office, thought can be given to building in such things as plant troughs in place of windowsills; tiled sills, which do not mark if water is accidentally spilt on them; and sills wide enough to carry a tray on which to stand plants.

SUNNY WINDOWS

Windows that receive direct summer sun can be used for some flowering plants and succulents. From October to March in Britain the sun is not normally strong enough to damage plants and many may be placed in

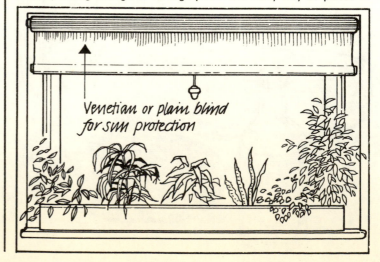

Venetian or plain blind for sun protection

a south- or west-facing window. During summer however such a window may need a thin curtain to lessen the strength of the sun. Alternatively, a blind can be drawn partway down inside the window or an awning pulled down outside. Failing this, the plants can be moved elsewhere for the summer.

Outside awning for sun protection of a south facing window

TURNING PLANTS

Leaves tend to turn towards the light, so sometimes plants need to be turned the opposite way round so that they keep a good shape and get adequate and even light.

PLACING PLANTS AT DIFFERENT LEVELS

To take advantage of as much window light as possible a variety of levels can be achieved with the use of wall brackets, glass shelves, transparent Perspex stands or glass bricks on which to stand pots.

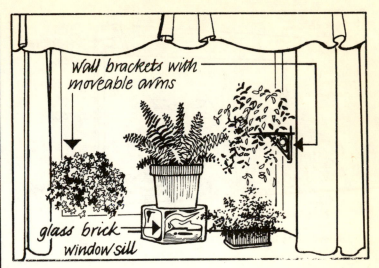

Wall brackets with moveable arms

glass brick window sill

ARTIFICIAL LIGHT

Artificial light can be used to supplement natural light where little is available. It can also be used as the only lighting where plants would improve a dark corner. Spotlights with a filament bulb can generate so much heat that the plants will be scorched unless the lights are placed several feet from the plants; warm fluorescent strip lighting is much safer and should be installed at least 12 inches above the tops of the plants and preferably about 2½ to 3 feet. It is advisable to have plants of similar height so that all can receive the same amount of light.

A period of full darkness is essential to all plants but the artificial lighting should be on for about twelve hours in twenty-four.

Some plants are more suitable than others for growing under lights (see chart on p. 13). Experiment will be necessary for a while to find the best plants for the selected position. If leaves curl up the light should be lifted or the plant lowered. If stems elongate then the light is too far from the plants and should be altered.

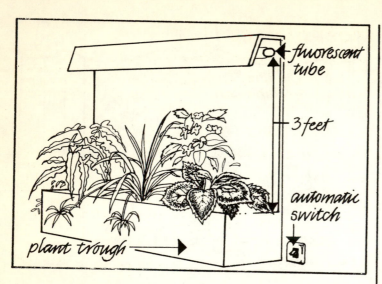

fluorescent tube

3 feet

automatic switch

plant trough →

A GUIDE TO PLANTS FOR DIFFERENT LIGHTING

DIRECT SUN IN WINTER

Azalea	*Coleus*	*Kalanchoë*
bay	*Echeveria*	passion flower
Beloperone	*Fatshedera*	*Poinsettia*
cacti	geranium	*Primula*
Chrysanthemum	*Hoya*	*Sedum*
Cobaea	*Impatiens*	*Sempervivum*
	Jasmine	succulents

SOME WINTER SUN

African violet	geranium	*Sansevieria*
Chlorophytum	*Peperomia*	variegated ivies
flowering plants	rubber plant	

VERY LIGHT BUT SUNLESS
such as an east or north windowsill

Ananas	*Fuchsia*	*Rhoicissus*
Begonia	geranium	rubber plant
Billbergia	*Gloxinia*	*Sansevieria*
Chlorophytum	*Hydrangea*	*Schefflera*
Christmas cactus	*Monstera*	*Tradescantia*
Cissus	*Pilea*	variegated ivies
Cyclamen	plants with	
Fatsia	variegated leaves	

MEDIUM LIGHT
light from a window but not a windowsill

R*Aspidistra*	*Chlorophytum*	*Cissus*
ferns	*Maranta*	*Monstera*
Peperomia	*Philodendron*	*Schefflera*

LOW LIGHT; SHADE

Aspidistra	ferns	*Peperomia*
Araucaria	ivies	*Philodendron*
Fatshedera	*Maranta*	rubber plant
Fatsia	*Monstera*	*Sansevieria*
		Schefflera

ARTIFICIAL LIGHT

African violet	Gloxinia	Philodendron
Beloperone	Hoya	Pilea
Coleus	Kalanchoë	Sansevieria
Fuchsia	Impatiens	Sedum

TEMPERATURE

The second condition to consider after the available light is the temperature of the room. Most house plants are descended from plants of the tropics but this does not mean they need to live in a high temperature. In fact very few grow well in temperatures over 75°F. This means that a very warm, dry, living room can be too hot for many plants. Most people keep their homes and offices at under 75°F for working purposes so plants grow well in the normal temperatures enjoyed by people.

Plants can stand higher temperatures out of doors in tropical climates because more moisture and light are available. Indoors the light and humidity are less, so the temperature needs to be less also.

A fairly constant moderate temperature is ideal and most plants grow well in temperatures between 50° and 65°F. In a room warmer than 65°F the coolest place in the room should be found for a plant—probably near a window. Few rooms have a constant temperature throughout.

plants should be on the room side of a curtain in cold weather

FROST DAMAGE

The window of an unheated room may be too cold at night for plants, so they should be moved nearer to the centre of the room temporarily. They should always be kept on the room side of the curtain and not on the window side when the curtain is drawn—this protects them from cold and also from sudden drops in temperature.

FLUCTUATING TEMPERATURES

Some homes, and many shops and offices, are warm during the day and cold at night when central heating is turned off. As long as the rooms are frost-proof there are many plants that can survive a drop in temperature, but a sudden drop of more than fifteen degrees may kill them. If this can be anticipated plants should be moved to the centre of a room overnight or a piece of newspaper placed over each one. Some plants can take fluctuating temperatures better than others.

A GUIDE TO PLANTS REQUIRING DIFFERENT TEMPERATURES

NO WINTER HEAT

cold but frost proof

Araucaria	Cissus	Hydrangea
Aspidistra	Fatshedera	ivies
Aucuba	Fatsia	Saxifraga
bay	Fuchsia	Sedum
Billbergia	Grevillea	Tradescantia
		Zebrina

MINIMUM TEMPERATURE 45°–50°F

Azalea	Heptapleurum	Plumbago
Beloperone	Impatiens	Rhoicissus
Chlorophytum	Philodendron	rubber plant
Echeveria	Pilea	Sansevieria
geranium		Zebrina

MINIMUM TEMPERATURE 50°–55°F

Ananas
Begonia
Christmas cactus
Chrysanthemum
Cobaea
Coleus
Cyclamen
Gloxinia

Gynura
Hibiscus
Hoya
Kalanchoë
Kentia
Ipomoea
Maranta
Monstera

Neanthe bella
oleander
Peperomia
Primula
Ricinus
Schefflera
Solanum
Stephanotis

MINIMUM TEMPERATURE 60°F

Aechmea
African violet

Cryptanthus
Poinsettia

FLUCTUATING TEMPERATURES

will survive but not thrive

Hoya

Monstera

Philodendron
    bipinnatifidum
Philodendron
    scandens

rubber plant

Tradescantia

CONTINUOUS WARMTH

central heating for twenty-four hours

African violet
Aspidistra
Begonia rex
Billbergia
Cryptanthus

Hoya
Maranta
Monstera
Peperomia
Philodendron

Pilea
Rhoicissus
rubber plant
Sansevieria
Tradescantia
Zebrina

TEMPERATURE CONVERSION TABLE

°F	°C	°F	°C	°F	°C	°F	°C
100	37·8	82	27·8	65	18·3	48	8·9
99	37·2	81	27·2	64	17·8	47	8·3
98	36·7	80	26·7	63	17·2	46	7·8
97	36·1	79	26·1	62	16·7	45	7·2
96	35·6	78	25·6	61	16·1	44	6·7
95	35·0	77	25·0	60	15·6	43	6·1
94	34·4	76	24·4	59	15·0	42	5·6
93	33·9	75	23·9	58	14·4	41	5·0
92	33·3	74	23·3	57	13·9	40	4·4
91	32·8	73	22·8	56	13·3	39	3·9
90	32·2	72	22·2	55	12·8	38	3·3
89	31·7	71	21·7	54	12·2	37	2·8
88	31·1	70	21·1	53	11·7	36	2·2
87	30·6	69	20·6	52	11·1	35	1·7
86	30·0	68	20·0	51	10·6	34	1·1
85	29·4	67	19·4	50	10·0	33	0·6
84	28·9	66	18·9	49	9·4	32	0·0
83	28·3						(freezing)

DRY ATMOSPHERE

Aechmea
Aspidistra
Billbergia
cacti
Chlorophytum
Grevillea

Hoya
Neanthe bella
Philodendron scandens
Philodendron
    bippinatifidum
Pilea

rubber plant
Sansevieria
Sedum
succulents
Tradescantia
Zebrina

FUMES

Most plants do not thrive where there are fumes from a gas fire, tobacco or intensive cooking. A few are tolerant of fumes but do better when there is ventilation. Opening a window sometimes will probably be better for the plants and for the occupants of the room.

PLANTS TOLERANT OF FUMES

tobacco, cooking, gas

Aechmea	Cissus	rubber plant
Araucaria	Hoya	Sansevieria
Aspidistra	Monstera	Schefflera
Aucuba	Philodendron	Tradescantia
Billbergia	scandens	Zebrina

The thicker-leafed plants do better here but no flowering plants like fumes.

WATER

Once the plant has been positioned in a place which suits as near as possible its requirements in relation to light and temperature then its other needs—water, food and humidity—must be considered. It would be so easy if every plant needed half a pint of water once a week, food fortnightly and spraying every three weeks. But this is not so and plants vary considerably in their needs—as do people. For example, some plants need water once a week, others once a month and so on.

It can be a mistake for the beginner to buy a large number of plants at once and it is better to buy one or two to begin with. The differing requirements can be confusing and it is easier to learn the needs of one or two before buying other varieties.

Correct care is simply a matter of learning the basic appetites of each plant when growing in the special conditions of your home or office. For example, the same plant may need more water in another home because the air is drier.

A seedling in sandy soil may need water every day but a cactus used to desert conditions may not need it for months. A plant in a warm living room with dry air may need frequent watering but the same plant in a cool bedroom will need less water. Normally more water is needed by all plants in the summer.

Water is needed in the soil in which the plant has its roots: it is also needed in the surrounding atmosphere.

RESTING PERIODS

Plants need periods of rest, but not for certain hours in every 24, as with people: rest is needed for several weeks at a time. Normally this is between October and March, and growth slows down during this time. Less food and water, and less warmth in the case of some plants, are needed at this time.

WATERING THE SOIL

Fill the space between the top of the soil and the rim of the pot with water, pouring with the long narrow spout of the watering can *on to the soil*, and not on to the plant. If water does not drain right through the holes in the bottom of the pot, fill the space again. Overflow water standing in the plant pot saucer or the outer decorative pot may be left if there is not a lot of it. It should soon evaporate. Excessive amounts should be poured away as otherwise the soil will become soggy in the bottom of the plant pot and the roots of the plant may rot.

An occasional good soaking is very much better for the plant than a daily dribble. Forgetting to water plants is rarely a disaster but over-watering—that is, keeping the soil constantly soggy—is the biggest killer of house plants.

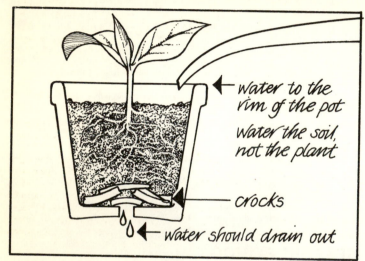

water to the rim of the pot

water the soil, not the plant

crocks

water should drain out

SIGNS THAT WATER IS NEEDED

Look for the following signs:
The soil looks grey—moist soil is darker.
When pressed the soil does not feel sticky to the finger.
The soil seems dusty.
The pot feels very much lighter than it does after watering.
The surface is hard-baked and possibly cracked.
Under the surface, the soil seems dry.
The plant wilts. (This normally does little harm except to a *Hydrangea* or *Azalea*. After watering the plant revives in a few hours. Harm may be done if a plant *often* has to signal the need for water by wilting.)
The pot when tapped gives a clear ring and not a dull thud which shows a pot full of water (this does not apply to plastic pots).

VERY DRY SOIL

If circumstances have caused the soil to dry rock-hard, water applied to the top of the soil may run straight off. It is better in this case to place the plant pot in a bucket or sink of water and leave it until the bubbles stop rising.

WATER TEMPERATURE

Tepid water—that is, water that does not feel chilly to the hand—is best for plants. Tap water is quite satisfactory but if rain water is available it is beneficial, especially if the water from the tap is hard, because hard water causes lime to build up in the pot.

WATERING FROM BELOW

Cyclamen, Gloxinia and African violets soon rot if water lies between the leaves and the crown from which the flowers grow. They are better watered by standing the pot in a saucer of water until the soil is moist. Pour excess water away.

CONDITIONS THAT AFFECT WATERING
THE GROWING SEASON
Plants need more water while growing, usually between March and October, than when resting from November to the end of February or so. Growth slows down and sometimes stops in the winter and the amount of water given should be reduced accordingly. A plant that needs water once a week in the summer may need it only once a month in the winter.

POTS
Small pots dry out more quickly than larger ones, and clay pots, which are porous, dry out more quickly than plastic pots. When a plant is pot-bound—which means that the pot is full of roots, there is less room for water so the plant must be watered more often.

ATMOSPHERE

Plants in a dry atmosphere – for example a room with central heating – will need more water than those in a cool room or in damper air.

TYPE OF PLANT

Plants vary in their need for water according to the variety and the size. Fleshy-leafed plants such as succulents and cacti need very much less water because they store it in their leaves. Over-watering makes them soggy and then they rot away. *Sansevieria* (Mother-in-law's Tongue) is an important example of a plant that needs a minimum of watering.

Plants with many flower buds or young leaves need more water. Hanging plants are more exposed to warm dry air than plants that stand on the floor and so need more water. (A good way to water a hanging plant that is too high for the watering can is to place a few ice cubes on the soil. These will slowly melt on to the soil.)

The general watering requirements for each variety of plant are shown under the individual plant listings, pp. 65–96. However, this should be adapted to the conditions existing in the home or office.

WHY CAN A PLANT BE OVER-WATERED?

The roots of a plant take in water and nutrients from the soil. These travel up the plant through the stem to the leaves. The roots have minute feeding hairs called root hairs which work properly only if there is air as well as water in the soil. As the soil dries slightly air enters the soil and this stimulates the root hairs by providing them with oxygen. This causes them to thrust out and grow in search of moisture. When soil is always saturated with water the root hairs die, usually from rot, and eventually the whole plant dies.

For this reason most plants need to have short periods of drying out between watering.

The length of this time can be determined only by experience as you and your plant settle down together. It will depend on the variety of plant and the heat and dryness of the room. A good guide is to avoid watering when the soil seems wet already.

UNDER-WATERING

Plants wilt when they are short of water. This is because the leaves are in contact with air which is drier than their surface. Dry air has the power of taking up water in the form of vapour (this is why wet clothes become dry when hung outside, unless it is raining). In a dry room, water is constantly moving out of the tiny pores in the leaves and into the surrounding atmosphere. This is called *transpiration*. When a room is especially dry then it takes more water from the leaves than the roots take up from the soil and as a result the leaves may wilt, shrivel and fall off. When there is plenty of moisture in the surrounding air then less is drawn from the leaves. So a moist atmosphere is beneficial to most plants.

WATER IN THE ATMOSPHERE

Water in the surrounding atmosphere is quite as important as water on the soil but the relative humidity of a room is rather a matter of guesswork. A really damp room is obvious because things in it mildew.

Coal and gas fires, central heating, a lot of sunshine and a lack of ventilation can all contribute to the dryness of the air. In the summer open windows and doors add moisture to the atmosphere but in winter, with windows and doors closed, the air is less damp. Bathrooms, kitchens, laundry rooms and hairdressing salons all have damper air then normal because of the amount of water used in them. Conservatories containing many plants can be quite damp because of the large number of plants continually transpiring. This is a reason why plants grouped together often thrive.

PROVIDING MOIST AIR

It is not necessary for the whole room to be provided with moisture: it can be limited to the area immediately surrounding a plant. The term used to describe this area is 'micro-climate', meaning a 'mini-atmosphere'. This is taken to an extreme when plants are grown in a bottle or under polythene, since in both cases all the moisture is held in.

House plants growing normally in a room can have the surrounding air made damp quite easily. Here are some methods.

1. Stand plant pots on a shallow tray filled with about an inch of small pebbles or sand. Keep the pebbles or sand moist. The pots themselves should *not* stand in water.
2. Group plants together in one container, in or out of their pots (see pp. 36–42). Each plant, as it transpires (gives off moisture from its leaves), helps its neighbour.

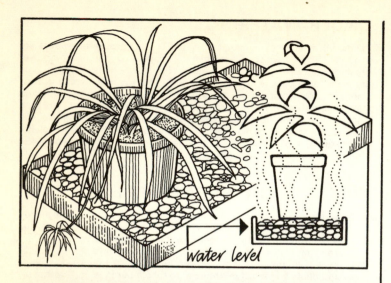

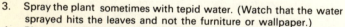

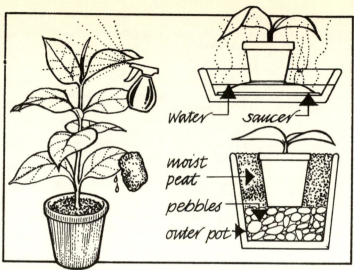

3. Spray the plant sometimes with tepid water. (Watch that the water sprayed hits the leaves and not the furniture or wallpaper.)
4. Place a saucer upside down inside a deep dish. Stand the plant on the saucer. Add water until the top of the saucer is just above the water.
5. Fill a larger pot, without drainage holes, with moist peat, sand, or sphagnum moss. Keep this moist at all times. Plunge the plant pot into this up to its rim. The peat should not cover the soil in the plant pot, otherwise it is not possible to see when the soil needs water.
6. Plants with strong leaves may be put under a bath shower sometimes and *gently* sprayed with tepid water.
7. In summer hardier plants may be put outside in warm rain.
8. Smooth (not hairy) leaves can be gently sponged about once a month or when you think of it. Use tepid water and a sponge, cotton wool or tissues. Some plants need this treatment to remove dust from the surface of the leaves (see under individual plants).
9. African violets and *Cyclamen* benefit from an occasional steam bath, especially when their leaves droop: place a saucer upside down in a deep dish; pour in boiling water until it reaches just below

the top of the saucer; stand the plant pot on the saucer for about five minutes.

DAMP OR DRY?

Not all plants like a damp atmosphere, but as a general rule those that require a lot of water on the soil also need it in the atmosphere. Plants that like a dry atmosphere tend to like a lot of light but not necessarily warmth.

FOOD

Plants need feeding if they are to grow well. There is food initially in the soil in which the plant has its roots but when this is used up more must be added. Only healthy, *growing* plants should be fed.

Plants are forced into growth when fed, so it is important to stop feeding during the normal resting or dormant time of the plant — if it is forced to grow during this period it will be weakened, as rest is necessary between growing periods.

HOW OFTEN TO FEED

Feed most foliage plants between March and October. Winter flowering plants are fed from November to February.

It is normal to feed every seven to ten days during the growing season but every two to three weeks will grow satisfactory plants. Even longer without food will not kill a plant, but will only make it less flourishing.

TYPE OF FOOD

A liquid food is easier to apply than a solid one. It is simply added to the water, and there are mixtures made especially for house plants. A few drops added to a pint of water are all that is needed. This can be done at watering time. The liquid fertilizer is a compound containing the essential plant foods: nitrogen (N), which makes good leaves; phosphates (P_2O_5), which is for the roots; potash (K_2O), for flowers.

Foliage feeding (spraying the leaves) is inconvenient indoors, and unnecessary for house plants. But if they can be taken into the garden or on to a balcony, it is useful to treat certain plants in this way.

HOW TO FEED

Manufacturers' instructions on the label should be carefully followed as they have conducted experiments to determine the correct strength. Giving more than directed could kill the plant so it is better to err on the side of less food rather than more. If too much is given accidentally, flush it away with lots of water poured through the soil or repot quickly in fresh soil.

Watering and feeding can be done in one operation as long as the soil is not very dry. If it is too dry pour some plain water on the soil before adding food, otherwise the roots may be damaged.

SICK PLANTS

A sickly looking plant should never be fed. It is better to wait until it starts growing again (just as people prefer light diets when they are ill).

REPOTTED PLANTS

Plants recently repotted do not need feeding for about two months as the fresh soil contains food. Plants potted into larger containers can last for as long as a year without further food. If plants remain in the same pot for a long time then food is especially necessary.

CLEANING PLANTS

Dust can spoil the appearance of a plant. It can also block the leaf pores and form a screen over the leaf which prevents light from reaching it. Sponging the leaf on both sides with clean water will remove the dust. It is difficult to sponge finely cut leaves and these are better sprayed.

Cacti, succulents and hairy-leafed plants should not be sprayed or washed; if it is necessary to remove dust a soft brush can be used.

A polish is available for the leaves of some house plants. This gives a lasting gloss for months but can look unnaturally shiny—a more natural appearance is given by washing with water. When using polish for the first time test it on a small part of a leaf and after two weeks look to see if the leaf is damaged in any way. In general, only plants with smooth, dark green leaves can take this polish. It should not be applied to any hairy-leafed plants or to succulents, *Cyclamen*, *Aspidistra*, *Peperomia* or *Kentia*.

Dead flowers and leaves should always be removed from plants.

CLEANING POTS

Plastic pots remain quite clean but clay pots may become covered with green scum on the outside. Steel wool or a vegetable brush and warm water can be applied to remove it and this will not damage the plant.

Pebbles placed in the bottom of decorative containers may need renewing or washing from time to time and the container itself may need a clean out once or twice a year.

POTTING, REPOTTING AND POTTING ON

Potting – placing a plant into a pot
Repotting – transferring a plant from one pot to another
Potting on – transferring a plant from one pot to a bigger pot

Plants do not need repotting or potting on very often and most grow better when under-potted. They thrive quite happily in pots that appear too small for them as long as they are fed properly and watered. Repotting is a disturbance that slows the plant up for a while.

Young, fast-growing plants may need potting on once a year. Older and slow-growing plants can go on for several years in the same pot. Once a plant has reached a 7-inch diameter pot it can stay in it for many years.

WHEN TO REPOT

Late spring (April to May) is the best time to repot house plants. If necessary it can be done at any time of the year, but plants do not like to be disturbed during the winter when resting. If repotting is done once growth has started up, the roots will then have a chance to grow and to become established in the new pot before winter comes round again. Some flowering plants can be repotted in summer after flowering (see Part 2).

SIGNS TO LOOK FOR

Potting on may be necessary when:
The stem and leaf growth are slow even though the plant is being fed in spring and summer; the leaves seem much smaller than normal; the roots are growing out of the bottom of the pot; the soil dries out very quickly and frequent watering is necessary.

To see if a plant is pot-bound 'knock it out' of its pot. If this is done carefully there is no damage to the roots. Place the right hand over the pot so that the stem of the plant is between the fingers. Then turn the pot upside down and tap sharply on the edge of a table. This should make the plant drop into the hand. This is better done when the plant is fairly dry – if the plant is watered beforehand the soil may fall off the roots. Plastic pots can often be loosened by gentle squeezing.

If the root-ball, that is the roots and the soil around them, appears to be a mass of roots on the outside with little visible soil then the plant is pot-bound and needs to be potted on. If there is not a mass of roots showing then the plant should be placed back in the original pot.

POTTING ON

Sometimes the roots may be so entangled that the pot cannot drop off the root-ball. In this case take a hammer to the pot, if it is made of clay, and break it gently, picking off the pieces. Plastic pots need to be cut off. When roots have grown well through the drainage holes it may be necessary to cut or break the pot even if it is loose around the root-ball, otherwise the roots can be damaged as they are drawn back through the drainage holes. Remove the old crocks (pieces of broken clay pots) or pebbles from the bottom of the root-ball.

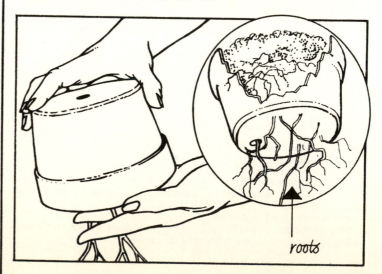

roots

EQUIPMENT FOR POTTING ON

Pots, clay or plastic; compost, bought in bags from garden centres; water; crocks (pieces of broken clay pot) for clay pots; newspaper or polythene on which to work.

POTS

Pots come in many sizes and are measured by the diameter across the inside of the pots at the top. They may or may not have drainage holes in the bottom. House plants need the type with drainage holes to prevent water from collecting around the roots. There are some tall pots for plants with long tap roots and shallower ones for the few plants that grow better in these. The pot in which the plant was sold originally is an indication of the shape that suits it.

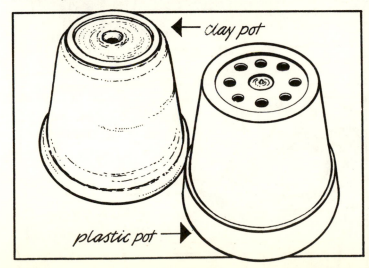

Clay pots   Clay is porous, which means that water passes through it in evaporation. A plant growing in a clay pot may need watering twice as much as one in a plastic pot but waterlogging is less likely.

Clay pots are cheaper and usually more attractive in texture and colour than plastic pots but they are breakable, and are not as easily available now. Green scum which can form on them after over-feeding may look unsightly. New clay pots need soaking in cold water for twenty-four hours before use.

Plastic pots   A plastic pot is much lighter and is less likely to break. The soil needs less watering as the pot is non-porous. Drainage holes are spread over the base of the pot (instead of there being one central hole as in the clay pot); this gives better and more even drainage.

Plastic pots are usually more expensive, but they are a good buy for the busy house-plant owner because the amount of watering is cut down.

COMPOST

The soil or growing medium used for house plants is called potting compost. Standardized composts for house plants can be bought in bags from retailers. The compost is ready-mixed, which saves a lot of trouble, and it needs no sterilizing. It can be used straight from the bag and is relatively inexpensive as so little is normally needed. These composts are based on sterilized soil (loam), peat and sand, with added fertilizers to give a balanced rooting medium containing the correct plant foods. Composts based on materials other than loam are referred to as soilless. Only with certain exceptions, such as cacti, should anything else be mixed with these specially prepared composts as the manufacturers have produced them for immediate use and to suit most house plants.

John Innes No. 2 potting compost (or similar) is suitable for most plants. (John Innes is not a trade name but the name for compost formulae.) Very large plants in 8-inch pots are better in John Innes No. 3. Garden peat may be added to John Innes compost No. 2 and 3 in the proportion $\frac{1}{3}$ peat to $\frac{2}{3}$ compost. The soilless composts are marketed under various trade names.

The few plants that need a lime-free compost include *Begonia*, African violet, *Hydrangea*, *Cyclamen* and *Erica*. A lime-free ready-mixed compost is available and should be specified. Cacti should be planted in five parts of John Innes No. 1 compost plus one part of coarse sand or in a soilless compost recommended for cacti.

PROCEDURE

SIZE OF POT

Choose a size only a little bigger than the present pot. The usual sequence is to progress to one about an inch bigger all round than the root-ball when this is placed in the new pot. In other words there should be an inch of space all round between the side of the new pot and the root-ball. It does not help the plant if, to try to save further repotting, it is placed in a much bigger pot: the plant will not thrive. Quick-growing plants however can make a slightly bigger jump in size than the slower-growing ones.

DRAINAGE

Plastic pots drain well as they have several holes in the bottom. No crocks are therefore necessary, although no harm is done by using them. As a clay pot normally has only one hole the drainage is not even and the one hole can also become blocked. A few crocks or stones placed in the bottom will give better drainage. A broken clay pot can be hammered into smaller pieces to make excellent crocks.

Place some compost in the bottom of the pot (over the crocks if used). Decide on the depth of this layer in the following way. The original surface soil of the plant should *not* be covered with fresh soil as plants do not like a change in the soil level. Furthermore, there should be room to water between the top of the soil level and the rim of the pot. If water runs off the top of the soil then it is too full. The approximate distance between the rim and the soil top is shown in the table.

Pot diameter	Distance
up to 4 inches	$\frac{1}{2}$ inch
4–6 inches	$\frac{3}{4}$ inch
6–8 inches	1 inch
above 8 inches	$1\frac{1}{2}$ inches

Plants that need very little water, such as *Sansevieria* should have the soil placed almost to the rim of the pot. This prevents over-watering.

Add soil to the layer and keep trying the root-ball in the pot until the desired level is reached.

There are two ways of proceeding from here.

Method 1 Place the ball of roots into the new pot holding the plant at the desired level (the bottom of the root-ball should rest on the new bottom layer of compost). Trickle handfuls of soil into the pot, shaking it sometimes to settle the soil down. Make sure there are no gaps at the sides and press the new soil well down with the fingertips so that the plant feels firm and well anchored. It is important not to press down on the *old* soil, as this may damage the roots of the plant. Bang the pot down to get rid of air holes and to settle the soil. Make sure that the new soil is level around the sides with the level of the old soil. Start again if the plant ends up either too high or too low.

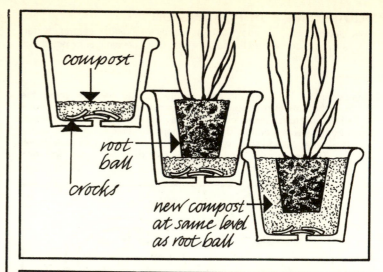

Method 2 After placing some fresh compost in the new pot place the old pot (having removed the plant) into the larger container. The bed of soil when pressed down should be deep enough for the rims of the two pots to be level. Fill the spaces around the old pot with soil until it is quite firm, pressing down with fingers. Twist the old empty pot around and then remove it. Place the root-ball of the plant into the remaining space. It should fit exactly and be at the correct level. Add soil if necessary.

After using either of these methods to replant, look at the bottom to make sure the drainage holes are not blocked, and if necessary clear them out with a small stick. Water the plant thoroughly making sure the water runs through the holes. Place the plant in a shady place for a week to recover and then return it to its normal position. Water again only when the soil is dry again—probably in a week to ten days.

CHANGING THE SOIL

Sometimes a plant responds to a change of soil even if it does not need potting on. Holding the plant in one hand, tease away the old soil gently from the root-ball with the other hand, being careful to cause as little damage as possible to the roots. Add some fresh compost. Firm back into the same pot. *It is important not to alter the soil level at the top.*

TOP DRESSING

Older plants which have reached their final pot, or plants that rarely need repotting, may benefit from top dressing. This simply means removing one to two inches of soil on the top with a small spoon, being careful not to damage the plant. The old soil is then replaced with new compost to the same level as before.

SUPPORTING PLANTS

Some form of support is needed for plants with long stems, weak stems, brittle stems, heavy flower heads, wayward stems and for climbing plants.

Artificial supports should be unobtrusive and should not spoil the appearance of the plant.

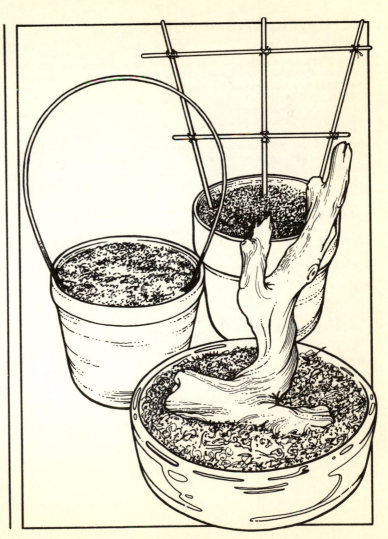

LIGHTWEIGHT SUPPORTS
CANES, STAKES

Bamboo canes and stakes for house plants are sold by shops stocking horticultural supplies. They come in many lengths and varying diameters. The stakes may be green or a natural colour.

Stake plants as soon as possible before the stems become untidy. Once out of control they are more difficult to bend back into position and often have deteriorated in the meantime.

Place the stake as close to the stem as possible and not around the edges of the pot, being careful not to pierce bulbs. A slender, pointed stick reduces root damage to a minimum. Push firmly but carefully well down into the compost.

Small climbers may be supported with several canes placed in the pot. Three may be placed upright across the pot, or two at either side may be criss-crossed with horizontal split canes or sticks, at 4–5 inch intervals, wired on to the uprights.

A hoop of very strong wire may also be placed in the pot with the ends pushed into the compost at either side of the pot. Finally, a tall, strong piece of driftwood may be placed in the pot. This makes a more natural-looking support and can be very attractive.

TIES

Ties can be made using green or brown yarn (wool, not cotton, which cuts the stem); garden string, also in green and brown; or wire rings sold especially for the purpose of supporting plants, and usually covered in plastic or paper to keep the wire from cutting the stem.

Rings should be placed around both stem and stake. Several may be necessary for each stem.

Ties are made by cutting a length of string and making a loose loop with a reef knot around the stem and then a second loop with a reef knot around the stake. Alternatively, you could cut a length of string and place the centre around the stem, cross the ends over and twist once or twice between stem and stake and then tie the ends together after going around the stake. The ties should always be loose around the plant stem so that the stem is not cut or damaged and there is space for it to grow.

Yarn or string may also be wound around several canes and stems in a web where there are many floppy stems, such as a bowl of daffodils.

HEAVIER SUPPORTS

Some climbers are self-clinging but others need to be tied to a permanent support. In the early stages a cane is all that is necessary but there comes a time when a more permanent, heavier support is required. There are several types.

TRELLIS

Trellis, wire, plastic or wooden, can be bought from horticultural supply shops. It comes in varying widths and heights in both square and diamond shapes. Colours also vary, and include greens, browns and white, so that the trellis can look as unobtrusive as possible.

Trellis can be fixed lightly to a wall with rawl plugs and screws or with nails. It can also be fixed to supports at the side and not against a wall so that it is free-standing.

WOODEN SUPPORTS

These may be part of the room decoration. Polished and stained lengths of wood may be fixed vertically between the floor and the ceiling. Pots or troughs for plants can be placed next to them on the floor. This is a good way of dividing a room.

MOSS STICK OR TOTEM POLE

There are two methods of making this very useful device, which is free-standing and does not need to be against a wall or other support.

Method 1   Buy a length of plastic wire netting, with $\frac{1}{2}$-inch mesh. It is 30 or 36 inches wide and this will be the eventual height of the support. Cut a piece about 10 inches wide and the full 30 or 36 inches and roll it into a cylinder with a $\frac{3}{4}$-inch overlap. Wire the overlap together about every 6 inches.

Place two sticks crossways through the cylinder a few inches up from the bottom to act as a brace. Place the cylinder (sticks at the bottom) on top of pebbles in a large plant pot or decorative pot or tub. Add some of the usual compost in a thick layer. The cylinder should now stand upright in the centre of the pot.

Soak some compost overnight. Squeeze out and fill the cylinder with it. (A funnel made of thick paper is helpful.) Keep pushing the compost firmly down with a broom handle or long stick until it is within a few inches of the top of the cylinder.

Plant several climbers such as ivies and *Philodendron scandens* in the

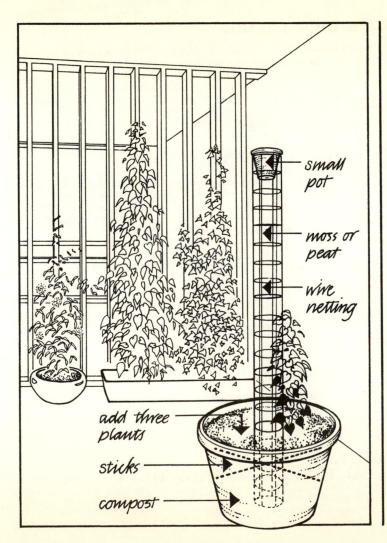

small
pot

moss or
peat

wire
netting

add three
plants

sticks

compost

pot around the cylinder. At first it will not be an attractive decoration but the climbers will soon cover the cylinder. If the stems need support press a hairpin over a stem and into the cylinder at an angle (or use a hoop of stronger wire for larger stems). The plant stems can be trained around the cylinder instead of straight up and this makes a better cover.

To water the moss stick, place a small clay plant pot on the top of the wire netting and fill with water which will seep down into the moss or compost gradually.

Method 2   Buy a 3—4 foot stake (or taller) with one pointed end and some sphagnum moss from a flower shop. Dampen the moss and spread it thickly on to a piece of newspaper. Place the stake at one end and roll on the moss, pressing it around with the hand.

Attach the end of a reel of wire to one end of the stake and wind the wire around the moss, about 2 inches between circles. When you reach the other end of the stake wind back again. If the result seems untidy roll the whole up tightly in newspaper and leave until the next day, when it can be unwrapped and should look tidier.

Push the stake into the compost of a large pot. Climbers and big plants that need support can be tied to this and the result is very effective. It is especially suitable for *Philodendron* and *Monstera*.

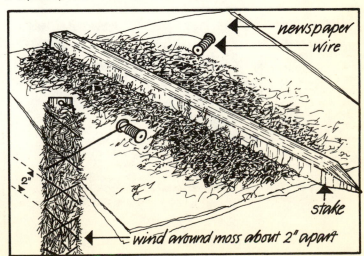

newspaper
wire

2"

stake

wind around moss about 2" apart

NYLON FISHING LINE

A really unobtrusive support can be made with nylon fishing line, which is sold for supporting different weights and can be very strong. It cannot be seen against a wall normally.

Knock a small nail into the picture rail and another into the top of the wainscot. Tie the nylon line to the nails, either vertically or diagonally across a wall according to the position of the nails.

Place a pot containing a climber on the floor or on a table next to the wall and tie the stems to the nylon or twine them around it. This is suitable for *Cissus*, *Rhoicissus* and ivies.

TRAINING PLANTS

It is sometimes necessary to shape plants by cutting parts off, in the same way as outdoor plants are pruned into a good shape. If growth upwards is stopped, the plant is persuaded to send out side growths and this makes a bushier plant. This is better done at the beginning of a growing period.

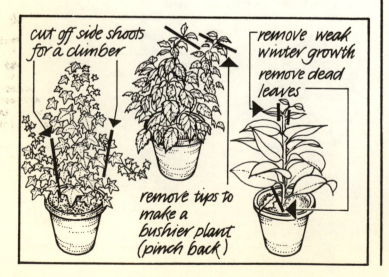

cut off side shoots for a climber

remove tips to make a bushier plant (pinch back)

remove weak winter growth

remove dead leaves

PINCHING BACK

This term simply means cutting off (using a knife, scissors or thumb nail) the tip of the plant at the very top. It is usual to do this just above a leaf so that a length of bare stem does not remain. This action encourages the development of side growth and stops plants from moving up indefinitely. It makes a bushier, shorter plant. 'Pinching back' and 'stopping' mean the same thing and it is a mild form of pruning. It should be done only when the plant is growing well. The normal time is late spring.

PRUNING CLIMBERS

Climbing plants need the opposite treatment as they require a good strong main stem and not side growth, which weakens the main stem. All the growing strength of the plant should go into making two or three tall stems. Cut off the side shoots in the late spring. The cut should be made cleanly at the junction of the side shoot and the main stem.

WEAK AND STRAGGLY GROWTH

Some plants put out weak growth during the winter. This should be removed in spring down to the first good leaf. Dead and diseased stems and leaves should always be cut off at once. Plants that get out of hand and untidy in appearance may be neatened by cutting off excess growth to just above a good leaf in the spring.

FLOWERING PLANTS

Fuchsia, *Pelargonium*, *Hydrangea* and *Solanum* bear flowers on their new stems, and the old stem should be cut down after flowering. However, *Hoya* flowers on the old stem, which should not be removed.

THE EFFECT OF CUTTING BACK GROWTH

The act of cutting the plant gives it a temporary check and so it needs a rest for a short time. It is better to reduce watering until new growth is seen. However any cutting normally encourages more vigorous growth and in time does the plant good. There are dormant buds on the plant which are part of its system of protection. These are forced into growth when the plant is cut. As this is hard work for the plant it is better that any cutting is not done often or drastically.

PLANT CARE WHEN YOU GO AWAY

Plants normally come to little harm if left for up to two weeks without attention, especially in winter. For longer periods other arrangements should be made if the plants are to be in a healthy state at the end of the holiday.

Pots are now available in a number of sizes and colours which provide plants with a reservoir of water. There are several varieties of design but basically the water is drawn from the reservoir into the soil as it is required by the plant. This ensures regular watering and is ideal for hotels, shops, offices and homes where the occupant is often away. It is not foolproof but normally quite successful. The pot may need topping up only once in three weeks or even longer. Directions for watering are given with the pot. Some of the larger sizes have castors to enable them to be moved around.

WINTER

Leaving plants alone in winter is normally less of a problem than in summer as the plants are resting and need little watering and no feeding. Water well before going away, and no more water should be necessary for two or three weeks.

It is essential to guard against frost: plants should be moved away from windowsills to the centre of a room. If the heat is completely turned off it is preferable to take them to a friend or neighbour for the duration of the holiday. This is also advisable for longer holidays unless someone will come in and water the plants.

SUMMER

This is more difficult, as plants are growing and need a lot of water. Hot weather can quickly dry the soil out, especially that in small pots. If possible, arrange for someone to come in to water well once a week, or

take the plants to a friend or neighbour (with instructions for care). Otherwise there are several suggestions:

Place the plants in a cool, shady room facing north. Never leave them in sunny windows. Water well.

Stand pots on a tray of gravel and water, and water the compost well.

Push the plants close together; water well.

Stand pots in buckets of well-moistened peat up to the rim. Water.

Put pots in the sink or bath surrounded with damp peat. Water.

Pot into self-watering pots.

Use any automatic watering devices available from retailers.

Cover with a polythene bag and place out of the sun; trap air under the bag and do not squeeze it out. Moisten, but do not soak, the soil.

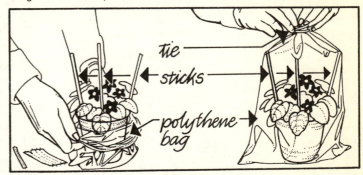

PLANTS FOR OFFICES, SHOPS AND HAIRDRESSERS

Plants can make such a difference to the appearance of rooms that contain only desks, chairs and filing cabinets. They help to create a more pleasant environment for the people who work in offices and to soften the starkness and austerity. Plants are especially effective in reception areas where they give a welcome and express a sense of care and interest.

Many office buildings now have an open-plan layout in place of many smaller rooms enclosed by walls. It is sometimes convenient to divide such a large office into several smaller ones, and plants are an attractive and flexible way of doing this without blocking out any light. They can be positioned on the floor or on top of filing cabinets or cupboards.

PLANT MAINTENANCE

There are contractors who supply a maintenance service for office plants. Watering, feeding and cleaning are normally undertaken. The service may include the provision of pots, troughs and plants, and replacements whenever necessary. Landscaping may also be offered. If no such service is available then the office staff are usually responsible for the plants.

OFFICE CONDITIONS

Conditions in office buildings and shops are not always ideal for plants. Some of the problems include:

Erratic care by office staff; too little light from small, old-fashioned windows; fluctuating temperatures with over-heating during the day and no heating through the night; dry atmosphere and (sometimes) fumes; no attention at weekends and perhaps lengthy cold periods (e.g. Christmas break); lack of facilities for repotting; too much sun through large modern windows.

SOLUTIONS

It is better to choose really tough, durable plants and to avoid buying varieties of plants that are harder to grow.

Mature plants are a safer choice and are cheaper in the long run than smaller young ones. Not only is the immediate effect more attractive, but there is a greater chance of survival.

Foliage plants are a better investment than flowering plants, which often look disappointing after the flowers fade.

Plants with leaves in a bold shape look better in larger, functional rooms than those with small, fussy leaves.

It is advisable to appoint one member of the staff (with an understudy for holidays) to care for the plants, so that a regular routine is followed. Ideally this should be someone who knows about plants or is interested in them. Clear, specific instructions on plant care should be given, preferably in writing.

Self-watering pots, especially the larger ones in which several plants can be grouped together, save work and eliminate concern over watering.

LANDSCAPING AND DISPLAY

The company's business is of primary importance in any office and plants should be placed out of the way of traffic. The movements of people should not be interrupted, and the plants should not be in a position where they are continually brushed against.

Plants grouped together in varying heights, either all in one pot or in several pots, make a more effective display than plants placed singly. This also helps to keep the plants out of the way of people. Furthermore, they grow better grouped together as the humidity around them is increased.

Plants placed above a radiator should be protected from the rising hot air by a shelf which preferably has a layer of asbestos on or below it.

When landscaping, water used in either a small pool or a fountain may make an attractive feature. Water also gives the surrounding plants moist air in which to grow and this is better for them.

ARTIFICIAL LIGHT

Artificial light could be used more often to grow plants in the darker corners of offices, shops and hairdressing salons. A time switch can be installed so that the plants receive about twelve hours of light. Plants that tolerate artificial light should be chosen (see p. 13).

HAIRDRESSERS' SALONS

Plants may look attractive and grow well in hairdressers' salons because the amount of water in use makes the air moist. Spreading plants should be avoided however as they get in the way. Most suitable are those that like a moist atmosphere and tolerate less light than normal. Ivies are especially good in cooler positions and *Kentia* is successful.

It is easy to spray plants with water regularly in hairdressing salons, but care must be taken to see that the hot air from dryers does not blow directly on to them as no plant will grow well in any kind of draught, hot or cold.

SHOPS

There is rarely room for plants in shops but more use could be made of them in shop windows, provided these do not face south or west. The best position is in the centre towards the back of the window as spotlights installed at the sides can be too hot for them.

GOOD PLANTS FOR OFFICES

Aspidistra   For cool, dim positions; medium size

Aucuba japonica variegata   (laurel) Good for entrances; likes cool air; large

Billbergia nutans   Easy; for dry air; medium size

Chlorophytum   Easy; adaptable; medium size

Cissus antartctica   Not for hot and dry conditions; stands fluctuating temperatures; climber

Cryptanthus   Adaptable and durable; small

Echeveria   Good for sunshine; small

Fatshedera   Cool, moist place; medium size

Ficus elastica robusta   A large plant to feature; durable

Gynura sarmentosa   Trailer; small

Hedera   (ivy) Where there is cool moist air; climber or trailer

Heptapleurum arboricola   Will tolerate high temperatures; medium to tall size; rapid grower

Hoya carnosa   Climber; durable

Impatiens   Easy; quick growing; small

Kentia   Tall, decorative palm; likes moist air; large

Laurus nobilis   (bay)   Hardy plant for entrances; large

Monstera deliciosa   Easy; a large plant to feature

Neanthe bella   (palm) needs little attention; medium; slow grower

Philodendron bipinnatifidum   A spreading plant for large spaces and featuring; stands low temperatures for a while

Philodendron scandens   A climber and good room divider

Rhoicissus rhomboidea   Easy; tolerates gas fumes; climber

Sansevieria   For sunny windows; little water; tall; narrow

Shefflera digitata   Large, feature plant

Sempervivum   Neglectable; stands sunshine, small

Tradescantia   Easy trailer; small

PLANT TROUBLES — SIGNS, CAUSES, CURES

If a plant dies it may be for one of these reasons:

over-watering: the most common cause of death

cold nights: especially if the plant has been warm all day

strong, direct sun: only a very few plants will tolerate this (the intensity of the sunlight is magnified as it passes through a window)

hot, dry air: such as a position on top of a television set, over a radiator, in a very dry room; or on a mantel above a fire

gas fumes: only a few plants can tolerate these (see p. 15).

lack of light: all plants need some light in order to grow

soil dryness: all plants need some water to live

Most plants naturally shed a leaf or two every year and the leaf turns yellow before dropping off, but this is nothing to worry about.

If a plant is giving some cause for concern, it does little harm to knock it out of its pot to examine the root-ball and ensure that the drainage is adequate.

Sign	Possible cause	Possible cure
Several leaves turn yellow and drop off (plants will sacrifice leaves to sustain the growing tip)	Usually over-watering; sometimes cold draughts, dry air or gas fumes; could be too low a temperature	Put the plant in a warm place to dry out if over-watered. Do not water again until there are new white roots in the root-ball. Alternatively, repot in new compost. Do not water. If due to other causes, change the position of the plant.
Brown tips and/or spots on the leaves	Usually the air is too dry; could also be gas fumes, over-watering, sun scorch or over-feeding	If too dry, spray the plant often. If due to other causes, move its position or omit food and water for a while. Keep away from television set, radiators, open fire and forced-air heating duct.
Leaves turn yellow but stay on the plant	Too much lime in the soil	Repot in new soil. Use rain water in place of tap water.
Wilting leaves, dry soil	Excessive dryness of the soil and/or air	Spray and water. If very dry, place the pot in a bucket of water until air bubbles stop rising. Keep in a cool place.
Drooping leaves with wet soil	Over-watering; bad drainage	See treatment for over-watering. Turn the plant out of the pot and add crocks. Clean out drainage holes.
Slow summer growth, pale leaves, spindly growth	Under-feeding; too little soil in the pot; over-watering, lack of light	Feed — or pot on if food has been regular. Give more light if in a dark place.
Leaves drop off suddenly	A shock, such as an extreme drop or rise in temperature; gas fumes; prolonged draught	Change the conditions if possible.
Variegated leaves turn green	Lack of light	Put closer to a window.
Frost damage	Plant has been too near to a window in cold weather and perhaps cut off from room heat by a curtain	Put the plant in a cool place and spray with cold water so it thaws slowly. In future cover plants with newspaper and move them away from a window to the centre of a room overnight.
Rotting at the leaf axil	Water remaining at the joints of leaves and stem	Water from below.
Water runs straight through the pot	The soil may be very dry and hard; it may have shrunk from the sides of the pot, leaving a gap	Immerse to soil level in a bucket of tepid water. Remove when bubbles stop. Press in new soil if there are gaps.
Water does not penetrate the soil	Soil too dry and hard	Prick the hard soil with a pencil or repot.

PESTS AND DISEASES

Pests are uncommon on house plants and you may go for years without any trouble. Cures are not as easy as prevention.

Prevention is a result of: buying good house plants from a reliable source; following the necessary cultural advice; catching any pests before they multiply; buying ready-packed compost and avoiding garden soil; throwing out badly infected plants at once.

It is thought by some people that a house plant should go on for ever. Pleasant as it is to own a plant for a long time, it is much better to throw out sickly looking plants, those with continually weak growth, the ones that are not suited to the conditions which are available, and infested plants. It is worth the effort to save large expensive plants which are especially loved but not small inexpensive ones. Most house plants are relatively inexpensive to replace considering the amount of pleasure they give and their decorative effect, so be ruthless and unsentimental and heave the plant into a bin or burn it. This does not mean that you are a bad gardener as pests and troubles can happen to anyone.

TREATMENT WITH CHEMICALS

Advice should be sought from the plant retailer as to the type of chemical to buy as these preparations are changing rapidly.

Insects will require insecticides; fungus diseases will require fungicides; and mites (not insects) will require acaricides.

There are also compound preparations, which will do more than one job. These products can be obtained in aerosol containers or in water soluble form, which is usually cheaper. There are some powdered preparations sprayed from a diffuser or the packet. Many of these contain powerful poisons which are intolerable to human and animals.

Always use chemicals according to the manufacturers' instructions and treat the plant as soon as you find trouble.

Spray *outside* on a still day.
Wear rubber gloves.
Never use more than directed.
Throw away any surplus.
Store away from children as many chemicals are poisonous.
Label the contents and add a poison label to the container.
Never use a soft drinks bottle for storage of poisons.

TREATMENT WITHOUT CHEMICALS

Whenever possible try methods of curing pests and diseases which do not involve the use of chemicals because although some chemicals are considered safe, they still need careful handling when applied to plants. The accumulative effect of chemical pesticides on the world is still not known.

PESTS

RED SPIDER MITE

One of the most destructive pests. It feeds on the underside of leaves and likes the dry atmosphere of a home.

Appearance
Tiny, spider-like when seen through a magnifying glass. A white webbing may be seen on the underside of the leaf and the upper surface becomes brown and brittle. Sometimes there are pinprick holes on the leaves.

Possible cure
Keep a moist atmosphere around plants if in a hot, dry room. When infected, hose down or sponge, especially the underside of the leaf.

APHIDES OR APHIS

Greenfly, blackfly; found in clusters on young shoots and under leaves in spring and summer.

Appearance
Small green or black wingless or winged insects about one twelfth of an inch in size. The plant leaves may be distorted and the plant itself weakened. They produce a sticky substance called honey-dew which attracts ants. Can cause leafdrop and yellowing.

Possible cure
A few can be picked off. Try mixing up a lather of soap (*not* detergent) in lukewarm water and swish the leaves through it. Rinse well in clear water. Try to avoid the soil getting soapy by covering it with a polythene bag.

WHITEFLY

Difficult to eradicate. A white cloud rises up when the plant is touched.

Appearance
Tiny, white, moth-like creatures.

Possible cure
Give the leaves a strong spray of

The larvae do the damage. On the stickiness excreted by the larvae a black sooty substance gathers on the underside of leaves.

cold water or try sealing the plant in a polythene bag for twenty-four hours. Either should kill off the whitefly.

SCALE INSECTS

Fairly easy to eradicate but messy. This insect draws on the sap of the plant and attaches itself to the stem or to the leaf veins.

Appearance
Small, still insect like a tiny tortoise with a hard brown shell. Multiplies and spreads rapidly and leaves a sticky deposit. The leaves eventually fall off.

Possible cure
Scrape off with a knife or the fingernail if you are not squeamish. Alternatively, rub off with a matchstick tipped with cotton wool and dipped in methylated spirit.

MEALY BUG

Usually found in leaf axils or along stems in the dark corners of a plant. It damages as it sucks.

Appearance
Looks like a dot of cotton wool and exudes honeydew. About one sixteenth of an inch long.

Possible cure
Apply methylated spirit on cotton wool wound round a matchstick. It is sometimes difficult to reach the bugs, however, in which case discard the plant.

In the case of precious plants that seem difficult to treat with success you might try contacting the horticultural advisory officer attached to your county department of education. Some local horticultural institutes may also give advice.

DISEASES

Fungus diseases are usually the result of a plant standing in a position that is too cool, damp and dark.

MILDEW

White mould on leaves and stems which looks floury. Often happens to *Begonias*.

Cause
Usually over-crowding or over-watering.

Possible cure
Improve conditions. Move to a well-ventilated position. Remove infected leaves and destroy. Apply a fungicide.

ROT

Rotting stems and/or roots.

Over-watering.

Keep plant warm. Do not water but spray if the leaves wilt. Water again when new roots appear in the root-ball.

IDEAS FOR DECORATING WITH PLANTS

House plants are very decorative and give life, beauty and colour to a room. They soften hard lines, fill empty spaces and hide shabby furnishings or plain walls. Plants can also supply a link in a colour scheme or give a lovely accent to otherwise dull surroundings. A room immediately looks lived in when there are plants in it and they can be a very economical form of decoration.

Plants are especially useful for making offices and schools more enjoyable places in which to work but they are also welcoming in hotels, libraries and shops, and can be used successfully in churches where there is plenty of light.

CONSIDERATIONS

There are various ways of displaying plants both in groups and singly but their artistic placement *must* be considered in relation to the conditions they need for healthy growth. They can then become a long-lasting decoration and replacements will not often be necessary. For example, plants may cheer up a dark corner but they will soon die without light, so you will have to provide artificial light in such conditions for them to grow well.

When deciding where to position plants it is important to consider the lighting and temperature available (see pp. 12–14).

Scale is important when considering display: for example, in a bare corner a large feature plant may be needed while small plants are better on small tables; windows may have tall plants at the sides but smaller plants are better in the centre so that the light is not obscured; grouping plants together is often more effective than scattering them about singly and one large grouping can take the place of a big feature plant, which may be expensive to buy.

THE PLACEMENT OF PLANTS

Plants can be positioned either on permanent, fixed furnishings or on mobile stands in a great many places.

WINDOWSILLS

These are ideal for plants that need a lot of light. The sill can be covered with tiles so that water does no damage to woodwork.

A plastic or metal tray can be bought to fit the sill. When filled with pebbles and water this makes an ideal situation for plants as both good light and moist air surround the pots standing on the pebbles. Alternatively, a trough, similar to a window box, can be placed on the sill and the pots can be plunged into this, surrounded by moist peat (see section below on 'Troughs').

When using windowsills there are some points to remember: the curtains should not be drawn in front of the plants on cold nights, as this cuts them off from the warmth of the room. (A blind may be pulled down behind them.) On a really cold night a piece of cardboard may be placed next to the window, or the plants may be moved nearer to the centre of the room.

Direct summer sun, especially through a south- or south-west-facing window, will burn up most plants. Only a very few species can stand up to this—mostly cacti. A Venetian blind, pull-down blind, or outside awning may be used for shading, or the plants may be moved to another place during the summer months.

Windowsills over radiators may be too hot unless a sheet of asbestos is placed on the sill. This should overlap the edge to direct the hot air away from the plants.

TABLES AND CHESTS

Plants may be placed singly or grouped on tables and chests. An outer, decorative container or a plant saucer is necessary for the protection of furniture unless the surface is plastic. Even then, puddles of water underneath the pot are not desirable. A tray, with or without pebbles, can be used for several pots together.

TROLLEYS

A movable trolley is excellent for grouping several plants as it can be wheeled to a window for light during the day and brought back into the room for warmth at night.

FLOORS

Large specimen plants used as features, and plants grouped in one big container can stand on the floor. They fill bare spaces and empty corners remarkably well and can be the focal point of a room.

It is sometimes necessary to move them in order to clean floors and their weight may make this difficult: a wooden platform with castors attached will eliminate this problem, and can easily be made. The platform should be the same size as the bottom of the container and be painted an unobtrusive colour. Some new containers are made with castors incorporated.

PLANT STANDS

Various types of stands, both traditional and modern, are made especially for plants. They are free-standing and raise the plants to eye-level, leaving normal furniture free for the placement of lamps and other ornaments.

Tiered metal stands

These may be found with several movable arms, each arm taking one plant. There are also tiered tables for holding plants in groups.

Pedestals

Pedestals with a small platform on top can be found, and trailing plants look very effective on top of them.

Such pedestals can be made from old standard lamps. Remove the electrical fittings and replace with a small wooden base, screwed through the centre to the top of the standard. The base may be painted, or stained and varnished, to match. It makes a handsome plant stand.

tiered metal stand

trolley for plants

tiered table

pedestal

wooden platform with castors

Pottery stands
Matching large bowls and stands may sometimes be found in various styles, but they tend to be expensive.

TROUGHS

(See section below on 'Troughs'.)

ROOM DIVIDERS

Plants can be trained up or along existing room dividers. If this is in the centre of a room there may be insufficient light for the plants to grow well, in which case a fluorescent tube may be installed to supplement the existing light. A trellis can also be fixed as a room divider (see p. 24).

TROUGHS

Plant troughs in wood, plastic or metal (with a metal or plastic lining), are easily found in shops. These may have castors or plinths or legs, or be made to go straight on to the floor or furniture.

A simple wooden one may be constructed at home and may then be stained and varnished, or painted. It will need a metal or plastic liner, which can be bought. Buy the liner first, in fact, and build the trough to its dimensions, as a standard-size liner is cheaper than one especially made. It should be wide enough for the biggest pot to be placed into it and deep enough for the rim of the deepest pot to be level with the top of the trough — pots standing higher than this spoil the effect. Remember that there will be a 2-inch layer of pebbles at the bottom. Smaller pots can be raised on small blocks of wood or inverted plant pots to the level of the other pots.

LINING AND DISGUISE

An alternative to using a ready-made metal or plastic liner is to line when necessary with heavy polythene. This is not quite so foolproof, as compost and water may get between the outer trough and the polythene, but it can be very economical and satisfactory. Cut a piece big enough both to fit the container and overlap the rim. Fill with compost before trimming off the surplus polythene at the top.

Brass and iron fenders
These may be bought in salerooms. They can provide an excellent disguise for plant troughs and may look very attractive placed against a wall or in a fireplace. Remember however that plants are in a strong draught in such a position and can come to great harm unless the chimney is blocked

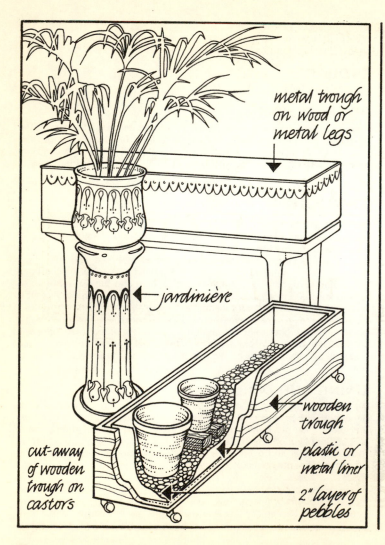

metal trough on wood or metal legs

jardinière

wooden trough

plastic or metal liner

2" layer of pebbles

cut-away of wooden trough on castors

up to stop any draughts. Lack of light may be supplemented with artificial light.

PLANTING TROUGHS USING PLANTS *IN* POTS

When you wish to use plants standing in their own pots in troughs, begin by placing about 2 inches of pebbles on the bottom of the trough. Sprinkle on a few pieces of charcoal which keeps the water sweet. Stand the pots on the pebbles.

Lift pots, if necessary, with blocks of wood or inverted pots, so that all are at the same level and at the height of the edge of the trough.

Fill the spaces between the pots with moist peat, which provides a damp atmosphere. Dampen it again when it begins to dry out. Do not cover the compost in the pots with peat as this makes it difficult to water. Plants may be watered separately according to needs.

Use some trailing plants as well as upright ones so that the edges of the trough are softened.

PLANTING TROUGHS USING PLANTS *OUT* OF POTS

When plants are taken out of their pots and planted in troughs, about 2 inches of pebbles should be placed on the bottom with a thin layer of charcoal on top. Then put a layer of John Innes No. 2 compost in the trough. Take the plants out of their pots and position in the trough, fill with compost making sure that the plants' soil is level with the top of the compost. Be sure to leave at least an inch of space at the top of the trough, below the rim, for watering. Firm down the compost. It is important to choose plants that like the same growing conditions, because they will receive the same amount of water, warmth and light.

PERMANENT TROUGHS

Permanent troughs for plants can be built into existing buildings or incorporated in the plans for new buildings. This should be done early in the planning stages. These may make really delightful features in rooms, and there are several ways of doing this. Architects will also suggest ideas.

Extend the brick of a fireplace wall to make a trough or planting bed.

Build a trough into a windowsill, omitting the sill if desired.

Make a plant bed below floor level, so that pots can be sunk down in peat, or plants without pots planted into it, at floor level.

A brick, marble or stone surrounding or edging is attractive, especially if close to a low picture window.

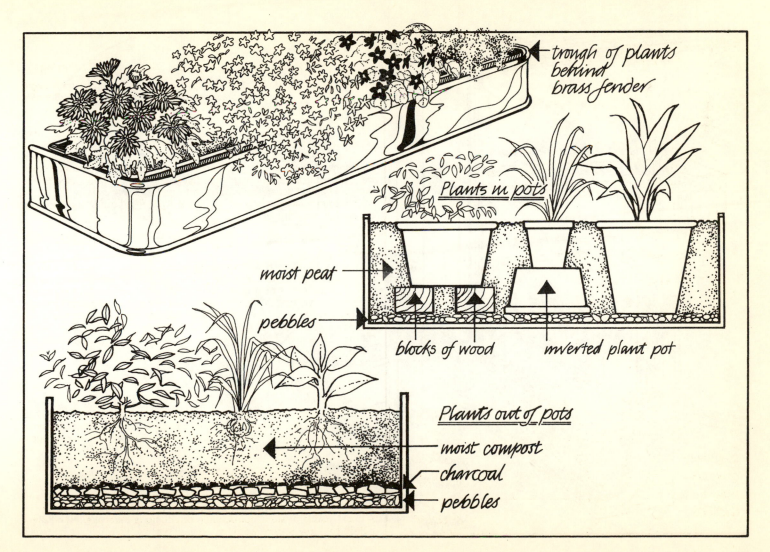

trough of plants behind brass fender

Plants in pots

moist peat

pebbles

blocks of wood

inverted plant pot

Plants out of pots

moist compost

charcoal

pebbles

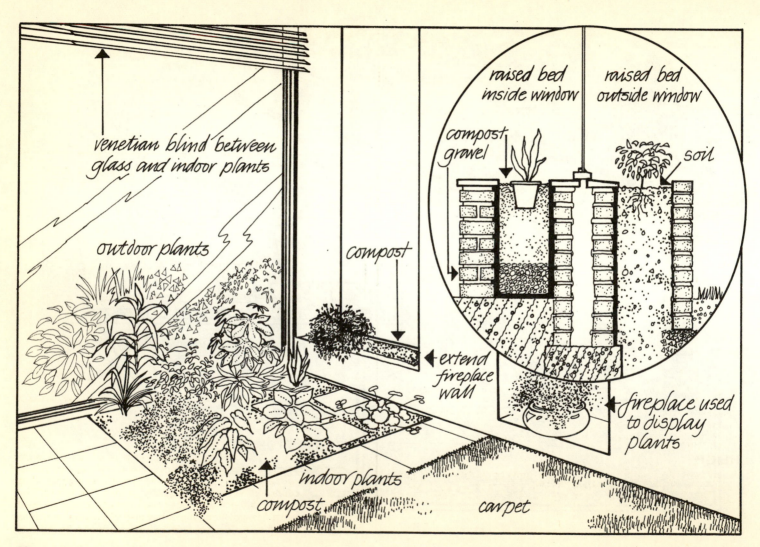

venetian blind between
glass and indoor plants

outdoor plants

compost

extend
fireplace
wall

raised bed
inside window

raised bed
outside window

compost
gravel

soil

fireplace used
to display
plants

indoor plants

compost

carpet

Build a brick or stone trough as a room divider.

An outdoor/indoor plant bed may make a delightful feature if troughs are built either side of a window at the same level outside and inside, with the window above. See inset page 38.

A plant bed can be made at floor level with a glass wall between. The plants are seen from both inside and outside with outdoor plants on the one side and indoor plants on the other.

GROUPING PLANTS

Plants are most attractive when grouped together but some thought should be given to their selection not only in view of their individual requirements but from an artistic point of view. This applies whether the plants are grouped together without pots or in their individual pots.

SHAPE

Plants with different leaf shapes look better together. For contrast, large oval or round leaves can be combined with longer thinner ones and more fussy foliage. Plants with foliage all of the same shape make a dull display.

TEXTURE

Some leaves are glossy, some velvety or hairy, some dull, some shiny and so on. There are many beautiful textures that can be contrasted in the same way as varying shapes.

COLOUR

When plants all of the same green are used together the result is uninteresting. A plant with variegated leaves brightens up the display and there are many plants with leaves in colours other than green. There are also many flowering plants with lovely colours. An all-green display has more interest when various shades of green are used together.

HEIGHT

Variety in height is also important, as low-growing and spreading plants soften the bare stems of taller plants. Trailers look attractive used over the edges of the container.

BOWLS

Plants look especially beautiful grouped in bowls and there is less of the 'all in a row' feeling of troughs. They can be planted with or without pots. A very deep bowl is needed if pots are used and it may be heavy to lift. The advantage is that the pots can be watered individually and plants easily removed if fading or overgrown. The disadvantage is that the pots may look heavy and unattractive and many people prefer to remove them for this reason.

The same method of planting is used as for troughs.

Plants in pots

gravel with charcoal — moist peat

GROUPING PLANTS IN BOWLS WITHOUT POTS

Some plants show their distinctive shapes better when not surrounded by other plants (such as *Heptapleurum*) and a few are happier living separately, but this is unusual. Most plants thrive when growing together, especially in one container, where there is plenty of moist air around. They may last for many years together, but of course it is sometimes necessary to remove one that has grown too big or has died. Flowering plants may look unattractive when the flowers fade and these can also be removed, care being taken not to disturb the roots of other plants. Some pruning, training and staking may also be necessary. It is not usually necessary to water as often as when the plants are grown in single pots, and this is a work saver.

There is one big consideration: *the cultural requirements of the plants*. All should need approximately the same conditions for healthy growth. For example, a *Sansevieria* (Mother-in-law's Tongue) needs a minimum of water and should not be grouped with a *Hydrangea*, which needs lots of water. These two plants must be grouped with plants liking similar conditions or left in their single pots and grown individually. The plants should

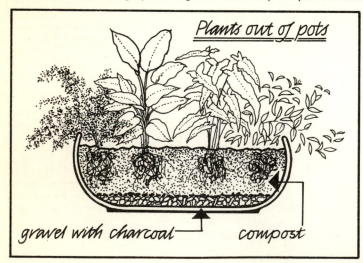

Plants out of pots

gravel with charcoal — *compost*

like the same amount of light, warmth, water and feeding to grow well together. Alternatively one must be prepared to renew regularly plants that do not like the conditions provided.

It is not as difficult as it sounds to find plants that like the same conditions as there are many which grow happily together. Look at the labels normally attached to plants in the retailers or read the notes for each plant in this book to find out if similar conditions apply.

Choose a deep container. All types can be used as 'bowls' including new ones specially made, copper pans, Victorian washbowls, and large vegetable and soup tureens. The important thing is their depth. There must

be room for pebbles, compost, roots and for pouring on water without spilling. They should be water-tight, but if not, a lining can be added or a piece of polythene placed under the pebbles. First, add pebbles to a depth of an inch or more. This is to ensure adequate drainage—excess water will collect in the pebble layer and not in the roots. Sprinkle with pieces of charcoal (from a garden centre). Charcoal absorbs odours and will keep the compost sweet. Add a layer of John Innes No. 2 compost.

Remove the plants from their pots (see p. 20). Place them with their root-balls on the compost. Arrange artistically with regard to leaf shape, colour, texture and height. Tall plants should go towards the back, spreaders at the sides and trailers over the edge of the container to soften the appearance. Some plants may be slightly tipped for a better angle and will come to no harm.

When satisfied with the grouping, fill the spaces between them with John Innes No. 2 compost and firm the plants well in. Leave at least an inch at the top above the soil level and below the rim of the pot for watering. Water.

The surface can be covered with moss or a few stones or pebbles. A piece of driftwood may be added for a climber's support.

The plants will arrange themselves after a week or two as they search for light and space and the grouping will then settle down and look more beautiful.

MAINTENANCE

The same care is necessary as for house plants generally but less watering and spraying are needed. The bowl may need turning sometimes so that the light falls evenly on all plants as they tend to turn towards the light and this makes the grouping appear to be leaning to one side. Faded flowers and leaves should be removed.

POT-ET-FLEUR

This is the name given to a grouping of plants with cut flowers added. The plants grow in the container and flowers are added for a colour accent when desired—if a small space for them is left in the centre of the container when planting, and a food tin about 3 inches wide, painted in dark green or black so that it is disguised, can be pushed into the compost to hold water for the cut ends of the flower stems.

For support a pinholder (lead with sharp pins embedded in it), obtainable from a flower shop, can be placed in the tin. An alternative method of supporting flower stems is wet Oasis. This is a plastic foam obtainable from flower shops which soaks up and retains water. A piece of this can be

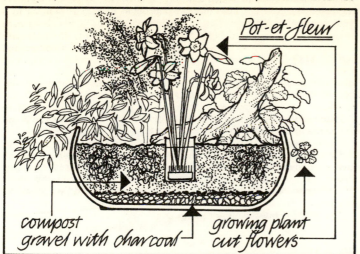

Pot-et-fleur

compost
gravel with charcoal

growing plant
cut flowers

cut from a block and soaked in deep water until it drops level with the surface of the water—this only takes a few minutes. It should then be pushed into the food tin (the pinholder is unnecessary); the flower stems, pressed into the foam, will be held firmly and accurately in position. The tin should be kept full of water, or the Oasis watered every day or two, to prolong the life of the flowers.

Pieces of driftwood, stones, coral and shells may be added to the surface of the compost for interest.

TYPES OF FLOWERS TO USE

Many varieties of flowers may be used with the plants, but only a few are needed. A bunch of daffodils looks lovely in the spring, three *Chrysanthemum* blooms may be enough in the autumn, two *Poinsettias* (burn the cut ends of the stems with a match to prevent leakage of latex) for Christmas.

Bigger flowers normally seem more in scale with the plants than smaller blooms. Lilies of all descriptions, irises, peonies, tulips and orchids all look lovely. Round flowers tend to look better than spiky ones. Before adding

them to the arrangement, soak the flower stems in deep, tepid water in a dim light for about 2 hours or overnight. Cut off a little of the stem end before placing the flowers in the water. Next day, cut the stem ends to different lengths so that the flowers will end up at different levels and group the flowers, which gives a better effect than when they are scattered about. Also turn the flower heads to face different ways.

BOTTLE GARDENS

A bottle garden is a group of plants growing in a large bottle such as a disused carboy or any bottle with a wide neck. Once planted it needs little attention for weeks and months on end and is a useful decoration for rooms seldom used, or weekend cottages, or for people who are too busy to be able to take much care of house plants but who like something green and growing around them. The garden is immune from draughts and dry atmosphere as the plants are protected by the glass.

A bottle garden is an adaptation of the Wardian case named after Dr Nathaniel Ward, a keen plantsman, who discovered in 1829 that tender ferns could live for years without attention in a glass 'box' with a lid. The Wardian case is sometimes called a terrarium.

When sealed, the bottle keeps all the moisture inside. The plants transpire through their leaves, the moisture condenses on the inside of the glass and drips down into the soil again to be taken up once more by the roots. Completely sealed containers can become steamed up and may not be as attractive as those with an opening. However unsealed ones will need a little watering sometimes when the soil appears dry or the plants wilt, but they do not need watering often.

THE CONTAINER

A large carboy, a glass fish tank, a fish bowl, a disused battery jar or any bottle with a wide neck is suitable. The glass should be clear to allow enough light to get to the plants.

TOOLS

Long-handled tools are necessary to reach down into bottles. A simple way to make these is to tie very firmly a table fork (rake), a teaspoon (spade) and a cotton reel (rammer) to canes or sticks. A razor blade

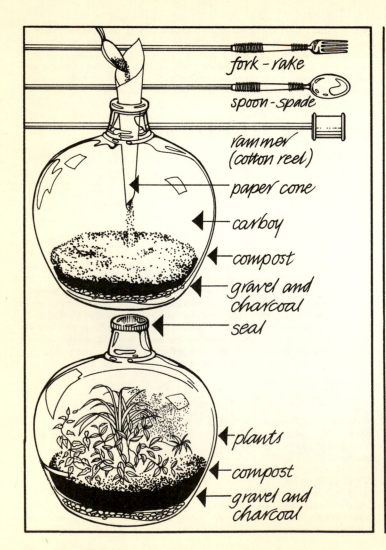

fork-rake

spoon-spade

rammer (cotton reel)

paper cone

carboy

compost

gravel and charcoal

seal

plants

compost

gravel and charcoal

wedged into a slit in a stick makes a useful pruner. A long steel knitting needle, or a darning needle tied to a cane, is useful for piercing and removing fallen leaves. Two sticks used as chopsticks may also do this job, if you can manage them.

METHOD

Clean the glass, inside and out, very well with detergent and warm (not hot) water. Rinse well. This will be the last clean for some time. Allow to dry.

Pour in a thin ($\frac{1}{2}$-inch) layer of peat. Add a 2-inch layer of wet pebbles. The peat will prevent them from cracking the glass. Drop over this a few pieces of charcoal.

Add some dry John Innes No. 2 compost or soilless compost. A 5-inch layer is sufficient in a large carboy. The sides of the bottle can easily become soiled again so it is better to drop the compost through a funnel made of stiff paper. Push the compost down with the rammer, add water (down the sides of the bottle).

The bottle is now ready for planting.

PLANTS

Choose small plants which are slow growing and varied in colour, form and texture. Suitable plants include:

Adiantum (maidenhair fern)	*Maranta*
African violet	mosses
Begonia rex (small-leafed)	*Peperomia*
Cryptanthus	*Pilea*
ferns	*Saxifraga*
Ficus pumila	*Saxifrage*
Hedera (ivy)	*Tradescantia*
Hoya	

Most flowering plants, cacti and succulents are unsuitable.

Try the design out first in a bowl of similar size. Then plant the bottle, starting from the outside and working in towards the middle. First make a depression in the compost where you want each plant to go. Then take up the fork-tied-to-a-cane and stick it firmly into the root-ball of the first plant. Tilt the bottle slightly if necessary so that each plant can be lowered directly into its depression rather than having to be inserted at an angle from the narrow opening of a carboy. (Obviously, with a wider opening the planting process is much more straightforward.) Tamp compost around plant with the cotton-reel tool, then proceed to the next plant. Keep plants away from the sides of the bottle and from each other to allow room for growing. Stones and moss may be added for interest. If the sides of the glass have become dirty, spray with water or sponge with a sponge tied to a long stick or cane.

MAINTENANCE

If the bottle is closed it will steam up for some time but may eventually clear. No water is needed for at least two months. It may go for a year without water but watch for drying out.

If steaming persists leave the top open. More frequent watering will be needed this way but a light spray every two months and watering into the compost every six months should be sufficient. (When watering into the compost, hold the spout of the watering can against the glass so that the water will run down the inside of the bottle and will clean the glass at the same time.)

Keep the bottle away from sun but stand it in a very good light and turn it regularly so that the light falls evenly on the growing plants.

A fish tank should have a lid but this can be left partially open. A sheet of glass can act as a lid.

HANGING PLANTS

House plants may be hung up by means of wall brackets and hooks in the ceiling. These should be used for only the toughest of plants (such as succulents, *Chlorophytum*), as they are exposed to difficult conditions. The air higher up in a room is much warmer and drier than that lower down, which means that watering must be more frequent. Hanging plants rarely die through over-watering! A saucer or outer pot is essential to catch drips and more feeding than normal is required. Regular spraying is helpful.

INCREASING PLANTS

Some house plants may be increased without much trouble in a normally heated room. This can give you a delightful sense of accomplishment and is an economical way of enlarging a collection of plants. It also provides replacements for plants that have become straggly and poor.

There are several methods of propagating (growing new plants) and some plants can be increased in more than one way. It is important to:

Follow the most suitable method given below; use clean, strong parent plants and best-quality, fresh seed; clean pots and seedboxes before using them; buy compost in a bag, as this is trouble free; moisten the compost *before* it is used; keep the air very moist in all methods.

RUNNERS

This is the simplest way of producing new plants, as in some varieties new plants form naturally at the end of runners (like a strawberry plant). Each plantlet needs to form roots before it can grow alone and this is encouraged by placing it on moist John Innes No. 1 compost in a 3-inch pot. It is essential for the plantlet to touch the soil and a hairpin may be used to peg it down. Roots should grow in a few weeks, and then the runner can be cut to separate the new plant from the mother plant.

PLANTS

Chlorophytum comosum (Spider Plant)
Philodendron scandens
May be increased by pegging down long stems every 2 inches in a pot, the stem tissue should be bruised where it is pinned down to encourage root formation.
Saxifraga sarmentosa (Mother of Thousands)

OFFSETS

These are young plants growing naturally at the base of a larger plant which may be removed when growing well and planted separately.

PLANTS

Aechmea (Urn Plant)
Remove when 6 inches long or with at least five leaves
Ananas (Pineapple)
Remove when six strong leaves have grown
Billbergia nutans
Cryptanthus (Earth Stars)
Echeveria

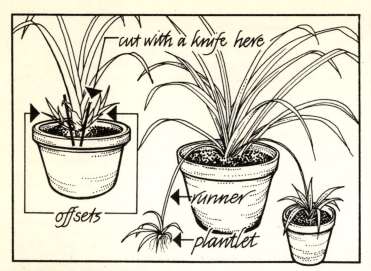

cut with a knife here

offsets

runner

plantlet

ROOT DIVISION

Another simple method for certain plants is division of the roots into two or more portions. This may be done when the roots of a plant fill the pot and repotting becomes necessary. Instead of placing the root-ball intact into a larger pot, it can be divided and replanted into two or more pots of the original size.

Spring, just before growth begins, or early summer, is the best time to divide roots. Wet the compost and remove the plant from its pot over newspaper. Shake away the soil so that it is possible to see where the roots join the main part of the stem.

Pull the plant apart gently into two or three portions, teasing the roots away with the fingers. If necessary a knife may be used but be careful not to damage roots. Replant the portions in pots of John Innes No. 2 in the usual way.

PLANTS

Adiantum (Maidenhair Fern)
Asparagus
Aspidistra lurida (Cast Iron Plant)
ferns

Maranta
Peperomia
Sansevieria
(Mother-in-law's Tongue)

CUTTINGS

Some parts of a plant, when cut away from the parent plant, may be persuaded to form roots (if given certain conditions). These parts are suitable:

The top part of a stem; portions of the middle of a stem; leaves; sections of leaves.

Any portion of a plant when separated from the parent plant for propagating purposes is usually called a cutting.

Remember that the cutting must be kept moist until new roots have formed as once separated from the parent plant it has no roots of its own for obtaining water. Some warmth is necessary and an even temperature of about 65°F is ideal for most cuttings.

TOP OR STEM CUTTINGS

The top growing tip of a tall-growing plant will root if it is not too young and soft. If it is, then it must be sacrificed and a lower section cut out. In some plants this lower section is better anyway. For example, rubber plant (*Ficus elastica*); wax plant (*Hoya*); climbing fig-leaf palm (*Fatshedera lizei*).

This cutting of the stem does not mean that the parent plant will die—given time, it usually produces new growth.

A portion of stem without any leaf may be used in the case of some

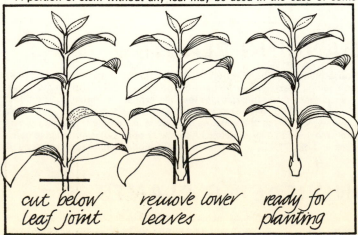

cut below leaf joint

remove lower leaves

ready for planting

plants but with others it is more successful to leave one or more leaves on the cutting.

Water the plant well before cutting and leave for a few hours so that the stem and leaves are turgid (full of water). Cut the stem just *below* the point where a leaf joins the stem because new roots will develop at this point. The cutting should be from 3 to 6 inches long, according to the normal height of the plant.

Remove the bottom leaf or two leaving at least 1½ inches of bare stem for inserting in the compost. Leaves on the stem should not be planted under the soil.

Put some crocks in a 3-inch pot (4-inch for a larger cutting) and add John Innes No. 1 compost, firming down gently.

Moisten the bottom end of the stem with water and then dip in a root-promoting powder which may be obtained from garden centres and other similar retailers. (The rooting powder is not essential for the growth of roots but is helpful especially with hard, woody stems.)

Make a hole in the compost with a pencil and insert the end of the cutting so that it presses down into the soil without any space between. Firm in gently.

Water but do not make the compost soggy.

Place a polythene bag over the pot holding it in position with a rubber band. This keeps the cutting in moist air which is essential, and in effect creates a mini-greenhouse. Three sticks placed in the sides of the pot may be used to hold up the bag over the cutting.

Keep the pot away from direct sun but in good light. In three to five weeks roots should have developed.

During this time fresh air may be given to the cutting by lifting the bag for a minute or two about twice a week.

After roots have formed the new plant must be prepared for normal living and the polythene bag should be removed for a slightly longer time each day for about a week to accustom the plant to room conditions. Then remove it entirely. If the plant wilts place the bag back again.

As there is little nourishment in the rooting medium the plant should be fed, *when growing well*, with a weak feed once a fortnight. When it has filled the pot with roots the plant should be transplanted into a slightly bigger pot of John Innes No. 2 compost in the usual way and treated as normal.

Cuttings from small plants such as *Tradescantia* look better when more than one cutting is placed in a pot. Five or six cuttings may be inserted around the sides of a 3½-inch pot. When left to develop, a bushier 'plant' is produced more quickly. If the pot becomes too full each plant may be carefully separated and transplanted into separate pots.

WOODY STEMS

Cuttings from woody stems root better if a 'heel' is left on the end. This is done by cutting the stem almost all the way through and then tearing away a small piece of the outer bark with the stem. Trim the ragged ends.

PLANTS

Aucuba japonica (Spotted Laurel)
 Autumn, 6-inch cutting
Begonia (fibrous-rooted)
 Spring, 4-inch cutting
Beloperone (Shrimp Plant)
 Spring, several to a pot, 3-inch cutting
Cissus antarctica (Kangaroo Vine)
 4-inch shoots, several to a pot, any time
Coleus
 Any time, 3-inch cuttings
Fatshedera lizei (Climbing Fig-leaf Palm)
 4-inch shoots, any part of the stem with leaves, any time
Ficus elastica robusta (Rubber Plant)
 2-inch stem section with a leaf, winter

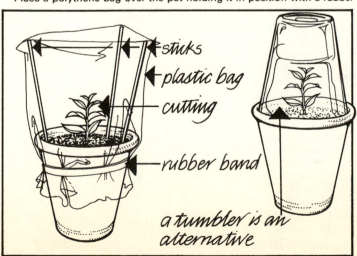

sticks
plastic bag
cutting
rubber band

a tumbler is an alternative

Fuchsia
   3-inch shoots, spring or autumn
Geranium (*Pelargonium zonale*)
   4-inch cuttings; dry out one day before planting, spring or August
Grevillea robusta (Silk Oak)
   3–4-inch shoots with a heel, spring
Gynura sarmentosa
   Any time
Hedera (Ivy)
   4-inch shoots, several to a pot, any time
Hibiscus
   3-inch firm young shoots in autumn
Hoya (Wax Plant)
   Firm cutting with two leaves, 70°F, and an inch or two of stem in spring.
Hydrangea
   After flowering or flowerless shoots, April
Impatiens (Busy Lizzie)
   After flowering or flowerless shoots, any time
Ipomoea (Morning Glory)
   Perennial, side-shoots in summer or after flowering
Jasminum (Jasmine)
   Cuttings with a heel in spring
Kalanchoë
   Spring, dry cutting 2–3 days before planting
Monstera deliciosa (Swiss Cheese Plant)
   Top of stem with aerial roots or a piece of stem three joints long, spring. This may spoil the appearance of the parent plant.
Nerium oleander (Oleander)
   5-inch cuttings, late spring
Passiflora caerulea (Passion Flower)
   4–6-inch cuttings with a heel in spring
Pelargonium domesticum
   3-inch shoots in spring
Peperomia
   Cuttings of short stem pieces with a single joint, spring
Pilea
   3-inch cuttings, five to a pot, any time, remove tips when growing well to make bushy
Plumbago
   3-inch cuttings in summer
Rhoicissus rhomboidea (Grape Ivy)
   Cutting with two leaves on the stem taken one half inch below the

lower leaf, any time
Sedum
   3-inch cuttings any time, any part of the stem with leaves
Solanum capsicastrum (Winter Cherry)
   April, young shoots
Tradescantia (Wandering Sailor)
   3-inch cuttings, five cuttings to a pot, any time
Zebrina pendula
   3-inch cuttings, five cuttings to a pot, any time

ROOTING STEMS IN WATER

Some top cuttings and a few leaves on stems will root in water without compost. *Tradescantia*, *Impatiens*, *Coleus*, and ivies are examples. This method is not always successful, however, as the roots, which have modified themselves to take in oxygen from the water, do not always readjust easily to the different conditions when later placed in compost. The cuttings will not grow indefinitely in water as they need the nutrients present in soil. New feeding roots have to form in the compost, and there is often little growth at this stage when patience is needed.

   Add a piece of charcoal to a jar of water to keep the water sweet.

   Cut a shoot immediately below a leaf joint and about 6 inches from the top of the plant using a sharp knife. Remove any lower leaves which would be under water. A single leaf of *Begonia rex* or African violet on a stem may root in water.

   When there are several strong roots, which may take from three to six weeks, plant into a 3-inch pot of John Innes No. 1 compost. Keep on the dry side until new growth appears.

HYDROPONICS

This is a technique by which plants are grown with their roots in water instead of in soil. The roots need to be anchored in gravel or similar material and nutrient tablets must be added to the water to supply food. These are obtainable from garden shops and the manufacturers' instructions should be followed. Although this method saves some trouble in watering is not suitable for all plants and any plant must be acclimatized to it from the cutting stage. *Philodendron* and *Monstera* can be grown successfully by this method.

STEM CUTTINGS WHICH WILL ROOT IN WATER

Begonia (fibrous-rooted)
Beloperone (Shrimp Plant)

Cissus antarctica (Kangaroo Vine)
Coleus
Fatshedera (Climbing Fig-leaf Palm)
Fuchsia
Hedera (Ivy)
Hibiscus
Impatiens (Busy Lizzie)
Nerium oleander (Oleander)
Passiflora caerulea (Passion Flower)
Pilea
Plumbago
Solanum capsicastrum
Tradescantia

LEAF CUTTINGS

Roots will develop from the leaves of some plants as well as from stems. Single, small leaves or sections of larger leaves can be used but in either case the leaves should be clean, strong and unblemished.

SMALL LEAVES

Dip the lower part of the leaf into water and then into rooting powder. Shake away the surplus and press down into a pot of John Innes No. 1 compost. Several leaves of, for example, African violet may be placed in one 5-inch pot.

LARGER LEAVES

Cut across the main veins on the back of a leaf (e.g. *Begonia rex*) using a sharp knife. Place the leaf face upwards on to damp John Innes No. 1 compost in a pot or seed tray. Anchor the leaf down with hairpins or cocktail sticks or weigh it down with a few pebbles. It is essential for the leaf to be in contact with the soil.

A second method is to cut a large leaf into squares or a long leaf into sections (e.g. Mother-in-law's Tongue) so that each unit includes part of the main vein. Dip the edge of the leaf into water and then into rooting powder, shake off the surplus and push the edge down into John Innes No. 1 so that a third of the leaf section is submerged.

FURTHER TREATMENT FOR ALL LEAF CUTTINGS

An even temperature of about 65°F is ideal. Keep the leaf cuttings covered with the polythene to hold in the moisture until new plants appear. Give a little air sometimes but replace the bag quickly.

Place the pot in good light at all times. Keep moist by spraying and watering the soil when necessary.

When new plants start to appear continue to keep moist. When well grown start to remove the polythene a little longer each day for about a week, by which time the plants should be able to adjust to normal room conditions. When the compost is full of roots, separate the new plants carefully, taking as much compost as possible with the roots to avoid disturbance. Replant as usual into 3½-inch pots of John Innes No. 2 compost.

PLANTS

Begonia rex
Whole leaves or leaf cuttings
Echeveria
Complete leaf with base attached, late summer; use cactus potting compost
Kalanchoë
   Complete leaf
Peperomia
   Mature leaf on a stem
Saintpaulia (African violet)
   Mature leaf on a stem section
Sansevieria (Mother-in-law's Tongue)
   3-inch sections of leaf
Schlumbergera (Christmas cactus)
   Young stems after flowering, dry for a few hours before planting
Sedum
   Single leaves

AIR LAYERING

Roots can be persuaded to form on a stem if the right conditions are brought to it. In this case only partially cut the stem in the beginning. The plant continues to grow with nutrients passing up the stem as usual. This is a practical and successful method of propagating tall, strongly growing plants such as the rubber plant and is one that has been used for centuries. When a rubber plant becomes too tall for comfort this method solves the problem and produces a new plant.

Spring and early summer are the best times to do this.

Place a tall cane in the plant's pot. Decide on the height of the new plant. The section above the chosen point should have at least three or four mature leaves growing from it.

Remove the lowest leaf. A cut is made about an inch below its joint. Make an upward slanting cut about 2 inches long. The cut should go about half way into the stem.

Bend the stem slightly as you cut and insert a matchstick to hold the cut open. Latex may leak from a rubber plant (this harms clothing only).

Stuff the cut with sphagnum moss or peat. Then wrap a handful of moss or peat around the cut (a helper is useful to hold this in place). Wrap the moss completely in thin polythene and seal at top and bottom with sticky tape or twine. This holds the moisture in and around the cut, which is necessary for root growth. Tie the plant stem to the cane to support the extra weight and act as a splint.

Continue to water and feed the plant normally.

Roots take a varying amount of time to develop—at least four to six weeks. They will eventually be visible through the polythene.

When many are grown the new plant can be cut from its parent. Cut the stem cleanly across just below the root-ball. Leave the end to dry for a day or so. Remove the polythene but keep the moss intact.

Place the root-ball, complete with moss, in a pot an inch larger all round than the root moss, containing John Innes No. 2 compost. Water and then keep on the dry side for a few weeks as this encourages further roots to form.

PLANTS

Fatsia japonica (Japanese Aralia)
Ficus elastica robusta (Rubber Plant)

SEEDS

Many people prefer to buy house plants ready grown rather than to start them from seed, which is a slow method of producing plants. However there are some quick-growing plants which are attractive in the house and easy to grow from seed, for example *Cobaea scandens* (Cups and Saucers).

Buy fresh seed, as a packet of old seed saved from last year may have lost most of its dormant growing power. Follow instructions on the packet.

Place crocks in a medium-sized clay plant pot (moist peat can replace crocks in a plastic pot). Fill with moist John Innes seed compost.

The soil should be about 1 inch below the rim of the pot.

Press the compost down with a flat piece of wood, or a lid, as seeds start growing better on a firm bed.

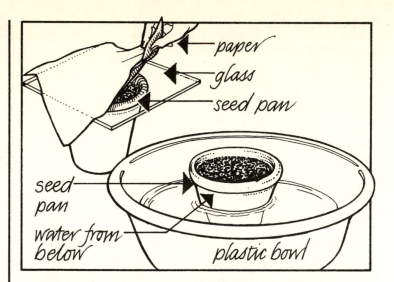

paper
glass
seed pan
seed pan
water from below
plastic bowl

Make some shallow rows with a meat skewer or pencil. Pour the seed out of the packet into the hand and then, using the finger and thumb of the other hand, scatter the seed down the rows.

Cover lightly with compost (sieved if lumpy). A general rule is to cover only to the depth of the seed. Tiny seeds should not be covered, as otherwise it is too much effort for them to push shoots through the soil. Press down lightly with the hand.

Cover with a sheet of glass to keep in the moisture and place a piece of brown paper over the top as seeds germinate better in the dark.

Keep the soil moist by lifting the glass and misting with a fine spray. Watering, if necessary, should be from the bottom so that the seeds are not disturbed. This is done by placing the pot in shallow water in a sink. Water gradually seeps up to the top. Drain well.

Water condenses on the glass and large drops can form and disturb seeds if they fall. The glass may be turned over each day or the water droplets wiped off.

Place the pot in a temperature of about 65°F.

When the seeds germinate, remove the paper and place the seedlings in a good light, but never in direct sun.

Light is necessary, otherwise seedlings become 'drawn' (weak and spindly) and never make good plants. Keep moist with the spray.

Slide the glass off gradually during the next week to accustom the seedling to normal living.

When a third or fourth leaf appears, the seedlings may be thinned out if crowded. Dispose of weak ones. Lift the seedling gently with a meat skewer and drop at once into a new hole made previously. The plants should be 2 inches apart. Firm in by pressing the soil around the stem (not the roots). When growing well transplant into 3-inch pots of John Innes No 1, transplanting into John Innes No. 2 when the pot is full of roots. A polythene bag may be placed over young seedlings after transplanting to avoid wilt, but this should not be kept on for long.

SEEDS

Cobaea scandens (Cups and Saucers)
  Early spring
Coleus
  Early spring
Cineraria
  April – June
Grevillea robusta (Silk Oak)
  February 70°
Kalanchoë
  Spring
Ipomoea
  One to a pot, do not transplant (annual)
Primula
  April or May for winter flowering, autumn for spring
Ricinus communis (Castor Oil Plant)
  Spring, soak in water several hours before sowing (annual)
Solanum capsicastrum (Winter Cherry)
  February

PROPAGATING CASES

Various sizes are available for growing cuttings and seeds. They have a clear plastic lid which is raised and has built-in ventilators. Bottom heat is provided with electricity.

GROWING HOUSE PLANTS FROM PIPS

It is fun to grow plants from the seeds of fruit eaten in the house. The results are not as handsome as the plants that are bought from retailers, and growth tends to be slower, but they give tremendous satisfaction.

The following will usually germinate easily:

Apricot stone
Avocado pear stone
Date stone
Grapefruit pip
Lemon pip
Lychee stone
Orange pip
Peach stone
Pomegranate seed
Tangerine pip

lemon tree

PLANTING

Choose the plumpest pips or stones at any time of the year. Wash with plain water and soak for a day to soften. Place the pip or stone into John Innes seed compost in a small pot. Cover with $\frac{1}{2}$ inch of compost. After watering cover with an inverted jam jar or a polythene bag and leave in a warm, dark place until there are signs of good growth.

The stones take longer than the pips—an avocado pear stone could take four months to begin growth.

FURTHER CARE

Bring the pot into the light and remove the cover. Keep watering and avoid direct sunshine. When a pair of leaves appears, transplant into a 6-inch pot with John Innes No. 1 compost. Feed weekly in the summer months when growth is strong.

CITRUS PLANTS

Lemons, oranges, tangerines and grapefruit need warmth but no heat and a damp atmosphere. They are better alone and not close to other plants. In the summer they need plenty of sunshine and fresh air. Pollination is necessary before fruits can appear and this is better done by an expert. A horticultural institute or nurseryman may do this for you. They grow slowly.

POMEGRANATE

Pomegranates have bright red flowers and grow tall. Water well in the summer and place in a sunny position. Reduce water in the winter to nothing and allow the plant to rest in a frost-free cool room. The leaves will be shed but this is natural. Repot in early spring in fresh compost. When new growth appears start feeding weekly.

AVOCADO

Avocado stones should be planted with the pointed end upwards in a 5-inch pot. Place it in a warm position during summer and in winter keep the temperature at a minimum of about 50°F. When tall it should have the top pinched out to induce bushiness.

SPRING FLOWERING BULBS IN BOWLS

Few sights are more cheerful in the depth of winter than a bowl of fresh spring flowers. It is very little trouble in the late summer or early autumn to plant bulbs such as daffodils, tulips and hyacinth which will bloom in the home or office during the drab winter months from December to March. With certain treatment bulbs can be 'forced', that is, brought into bloom a few weeks earlier than normal, so that they are in flower for Christmas. A bowl makes a very acceptable Christmas present.

After flowering indoors the bulbs can be planted outside for future years or be discarded. They cannot be forced in the house a second year. New bulbs must be bought for this purpose each year.

SUITABLE BULBS FOR INDOOR GROWING

Hyacinth are the easiest and bloom for a long time. There are blues, pinks, cream, white, yellows, red and apricot varieties
Narcissus, in yellow and white
Daffodils
Tulips including single early and double early
Crocus (the larger-flowered ones are best), available in purple, mauve, blue, yellow, old gold, white, sometimes striped
Irises, the dwarf ones are best
Chinodoxa, *scilla* (these small blue flowers are effective massed)
Snowdrops for small bowls

BUYING BULBS

Certain varieties are better for indoor growing and 'specially prepared' bulbs are available for forcing into early flower for Christmas. These will have been grown, lifted at the right time, dried carefully and stored at the correct temperature by experts to make them flower earlier than normal. The flower bud will already be formed inside the bulb at the time of buying, so it is essential to buy *good-quality* bulbs from a reliable source. Avoid buying bulbs with any rot and with badly bruised tissue. They should be covered with a paper-thin outer skin like an onion.

BULB SPECIALISTS

Garden centres and flower shops stock plenty of bulbs in early autumn and it is important to ask for the varieties most suitable for indoor growing. If they are required for Christmas, buy early (available from retailers in early autumn) and ask for bulbs especially prepared for Christmas flowering. Bulb specialists issue helpful catalogues listing suitable bulbs, colours, cultural instructions and advice on compost. Usually there are special offers of bulbs for indoor and Christmas growing. Rare or new varieties of bulbs are expensive and the best buys are the top quality bulbs of the more common varieties.

Narcissi (daffodils and narcissus) are graded according to the number of growing points on the bulb as each one should produce a flower. They may be:

single nosed: one growing point;
double nosed: two growing points;
mother: more than two growing points.

single nosed   double nosed   mother

STORING BULBS

Although it is better to plant bulbs immediately after purchase, storage will sometimes be necessary.

Unplanted bulbs soon deteriorate in warm air and are best kept in a cool, dry, airy place. If no such area is available, place them in perforated bags in the refrigerator but not near moisture. They should not be stored for longer than six weeks and never in the freezer or ice compartment.

If possible it is better to keep them in the dark as light may start the tops growing, like an onion. This is not an advantage as the flower buds will not emerge, the shoots having grown before the roots.

One advantage of storing is that a few bulbs may be planted each week so that there will be a succession of flowers instead of having all the bulbs in bloom at the same time.

CONTAINERS

Use normal plant pots with saucers or deep, decorative bowls without drainage holes. *The container should be at least twice the depth of the bulbs* to allow room for roots to grow downwards and to allow the compost to be watered. The tips of the bulb should be below the level of the rim of the pot and the soil level should be an inch below the rim.

GROWING MEDIUM

The bulbs already contain immature flowers and leaves and do not need feeding but they do need some medium in which to root so that they can take in water. Bags of growing medium are available from garden centres and other retailers.

JOHN INNES NO. 2

Bulbs planted in John Innes No. 2 compost usually flower again the following year when planted in the garden.

BULB FIBRE

This is very clean and light but bulbs grown in this may need an extra year in the garden before they flower again, as there is little or no food in bulb fibre. It is good for pots without drainage holes and clean for use in flats without gardens. Before planting, the fibre should be soaked well overnight and then squeezed out so that it is moist but not wet.

WATER

Water alone is suitable for a few bulbs but after flowering the bulb is usually shrivelled and is unlikely to grow well in the garden if planted out.

METHOD OF GROWING

Very simply, bulbs need a period of cool darkness for developing roots which they should have grown before the shoots develop strongly. This period compares with a winter in the garden and is the secret of success. After the roots are formed warmth and light are needed to bring the shoots into flower.

The information that follows is given in chart form for individual varieties on pp. 54–5.

PLANTING

Place a layer of moist, not soggy, compost or fibre in each bowl. It should be at least the depth of the bulbs. One variety of bulb to a bowl is better than a mixture so that the flowers appear at the same time. Set the bulbs on top of the compost close together. They can almost touch each other. No more than a pencil width apart is sufficient and a full bowl looks better.

Using the fingers fill the spaces with compost pressing firmly but not tightly, or the downward pressure of the developing roots will lift the bulbs. The surface of the compost should be at least $\frac{1}{2}$ inch below the bowl's rim to allow room for watering.

Hyacinth Daffodils Narcissus	Leave the noses of the bulbs just showing
Tulips	Just cover the noses
Smaller bulbs	Plant the tip just below the surface, about $\frac{1}{4}-\frac{1}{2}$ inch

almost touching · at least 1/2"

Water well after planting. Wash your hands or wear gloves when planting if you find the bulbs irritate your skin – some people are allergic to them.

The bowls should now be placed in a *cool, dark, airy* place to encourage the formation of roots and leaves. This is called *plunging*. It should be frost-free but not much more than 45°F. Suitable places include:

A cool, dark cupboard; a dry cellar; a shelf in a coalhouse; the garden shed; an unheated, dark attic; the garden.

PLUNGING IN THE GARDEN

Bowls may be placed in the garden, preferably facing north, in a trench or box. Cover with ashes or moist peat to a depth of about 6 inches. The bowls may be wrapped in newspaper to prevent them getting dirty. A cold frame or a balcony may also be suitable.

WATERING

Check the bowls about every three weeks to see if they have dried out. If they are covered with ashes push a finger down through the covering material to feel the compost in the bowls. If the compost in the bowls was well moistened in the first place only occasional watering will be necessary, especially if they have been plunged under ashes or peat.

MOVING INDOORS

When the tips of leaves are showing and preferably 1–2 inches tall, the bowls can be moved indoors or out of the dark place. This is usually six to twelve weeks after planting and varies with different bulbs. The leaves will look very anaemic because they have been without light, but will soon turn green when placed in daylight.

It is better not to put the bowls into a warm room immediately after bringing in from a cool place as they need to get used to warmer conditions gradually. A cool, light, sunless position with a temperature of around 50°F is suitable. After a week of acclimatizing the bowls can be moved into a warmer position such as a living room where their development can be enjoyed.

Draughts and hot positions, such as close to a fire, should be avoided and the compost (not the buds) should be watered regularly. The bowl should be turned sometimes so that the light falls on all the bulbs evenly. They then develop at the same pace.

Flowering usually occurs about four to five months after planting.

	Planting time	*Flowering time*
Hyacinth	September–October (early September for Christmas)	December–April
Tulips	September–October (early September for Christmas)	December–April
Daffodils	August–October (early October for Christmas)	January–March
Narcissus	September–October (early October for Christmas, removing from plunge by 1 December)	December–January

Crocus (spring)	September–October	February–March
Crocus (autumn)	April	September
Iris	October	January
Chirodoxa, Scilla	September–October	January–March
Snowdrops	October	January

DOUBLE POTTING DAFFODILS

A spectacular pot of daffodils may be produced by planting more than one layer in a bowl. Use a big, deep clay pot and add crocks for drainage. Fill one-third with compost or bulb fibre and place three double-nosed daffodil bulbs on top. Add compost to cover the bulbs. Add three more bulbs, setting their bases between the noses of the first layer. Fill with compost to an inch of the pot's rim. A third layer can be added in a big pot.

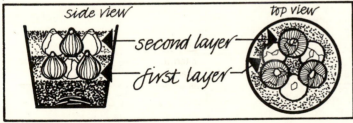

EXTRA BULBS

It is useful to grow a supply of bulbs individually in small pots. They transplant easily when beginning to flower and are useful for adding to bowls of mixed plants, window boxes and urns to provide a colour accent or contrast.

ADDING FOLIAGE

Small foliage plants such as *Saxifraga* and *Sedum* can be added to the bowls of bulbs to hide the soil and soften the appearance of the bowl. Moss is also useful for this purpose and is obtainable from flower shops.

STAKING

Lengthy stems and heavy flower heads need supporting. Small sticks may be bought for this purpose. Push one in next to each bulb – avoid piercing the bulb. Garden green string or yarn should be used to tie the stem loosely to the stick in one or more places. Another method is to weave the string in and around the sticks and stems like a web. The stake should be put in early, before the stems sag.

SUCCESSION OF FLOWERS

To enjoy several bowls of flowers one after another, plant at different times – perhaps one bowl a week. Another method is to bring the bowls in from the 'plunge' at different times.

Even though buds are showing above the compost the bowls may stay outside and come to no harm up to about four weeks.

AFTER FLOWERING

Remove the dead flowers as they fade. Do not remove the leaves or stems, as these feed the bulb for future growing, if it is to be planted outside. Finally discard the bulbs. If they can be planted in a garden move the bowl after all the flowers have faded to a cool, light place and keep the bulbs watered. In March or April take the compost, bulbs and all, out of the bowl in one lump and plant in the garden about 8 inches deep. If grown in compost they should flower the following year in the garden.

PLANTING IN WATER

Hyacinth and the paper-white variety of narcissus can be grown in water alone. Bulbs should be planted from August until November.

Place a layer of pebbles in a deep bowl so that they reach 2 inches below the rim. The bowl should be deep enough to hold the roots. A little charcoal can be sprinkled on to the pebbles to keep the water sweet.

Stand the bulbs on the pebbles and touching each other for support. Do not twist the bulbs in as this may damage the base of the bulb.

Pour water into the container so that *only* the bases of the bulbs are standing in water. If a whole bulb is immersed it will rot. Place the bowl in a cool, frost-free position until the roots have developed and the leaves

BULBS IN POTS – SUGGESTED TREATMENT

Bulb	Plant and plunge	Type of bowl	Remove from plunge
Hyacinth Christmas (prepared)	Early September	One variety to a container, 5-inch-deep bowl. Plant close together, noses above compost, not touching sides of container.	10 weeks later, in mid-November
Ordinary	September–October		12–15 weeks later
Narcissus and daffodils Christmas (prepared)	First week in October	Bowl at least 5 inches deep. Bulbs 1 inch apart (but may touch) with nose above compost.	1 December
Ordinary	August–early October		10–15 weeks later in January–February
Narcissus Grown in water (with pebbles) for Christmas (variety 'Cragford')	Early October: place in cool (around 45°F) dim light	Bulbs may touch for extra support. Fill container two-thirds full of pebbles. Container 5 inches deep at least.	Place in living room, end of November
Tulip Christmas (prepared)	Before mid-September	Eight or ten to a 6-inch-diameter pot, flat sides of bulb towards the bowl. Just cover noses.	About 1 December
Ordinary	September–mid-October		10–12 weeks after planting and not before mid-January
Crocus, *Chinodoxa*, *Scilla*, snowdrop	September–October	Eight to ten to a 5-inch pot. Plant bulbs 1–2 inches deep and $\frac{1}{2}$–1 inch apart.	8 weeks after planting
Iris	October	Better massed in a large pot. Plant bulbs 2–3 inches deep about 3 inches apart.	About 8 weeks after planting

Acclimatizing	Ideal living room conditions	Approximate time in flower after leaving plunge	Care in living room
Subdued light for a few days and low indoor temperature around 45°–50°F	Light, 65°F	4 weeks	Water well and feed once a week until in full bloom then lessen water to prolong flowering. Keep away from heat. Turn for even light.
4 days in subdued light, about 60°F	Remove to living room 5 December, full light, 50°–55°F	4–6 weeks	Water well. Reduce water when in bloom to prolong flowers.
Subdued light 45°–50°F until flower buds visible	Light, 60°F		
	Light, 50°–55°F	4 weeks	Keep water topped up, add a small piece of charcoal to keep it sweet – now and again.
In the dark at about 65°F until it has grown 1–2 inches	Light, up to 70°F	3 weeks	Water well, avoid bottom heat, draughts and direct sun.
In the dark with temperature no more than 60°F for 2–3 weeks	Light, not more than 70°F, no sun	According to variety	
Shade, 50°–55°F	Full light when green, 50°–55°F	Varies according to bulb	Plenty of water, keep out of midday sun for snowdrops.
Shade, 50°–55°F	Not above 55°F	About 4 weeks	Water well. Feed once a week.

have grown about one inch tall. Hyacinth should be kept in the dark but narcissus should go on a windowsill. Then bring in to a warmer room.

Top up the water when necessary so that the base of the bulb remains in water. When roots have developed these should always be in water. After flowering throw away the bulb, because it will not flower again.

It is not possible to stake when pebbles are used as the stick will not stand up; however, the stems may support each other if string or yarn is woven around them to hold them together.

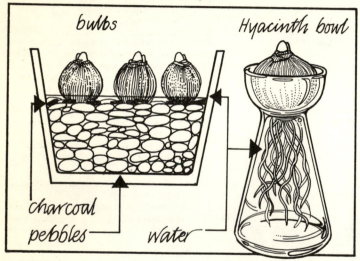

bulbs

Hyacinth bowl

charcoal

pebbles   water

SPECIAL CONTAINERS

Bulbs are now available in special packs complete with container to which only water need be added, according to instructions on the packet. Special glass bulb jars with a restricted neck may be bought for supporting a bulb in water. Hyacinth are specially suitable for this method. Pebbles are unnecessary.

SOME TENDER BULBS FOR INDOOR CULTIVATION

There are some bulbs that may be grown indoors but not in the garden as they are delicate or half-hardy. These include *Hippeastrum* (*amaryllis*) *Vallota, Clivia, Freesia, Nerine, Lachenalia*. Hardy bulbs can be grown out of doors and indoors (for example, daffodils, tulips). (The information below is summarized in chart form on p. 61.)

GENERAL PROCEDURE

Use plant pots with good drainage—normal plant pots with holes in the bottom are best. Place crocks over the hole in a clay pot. Add a layer of peat in either clay or plastic pots. Then add John Innes No. 2 compost.

After placing the bulb in position add compost all round the bulb and firm well in until the surface is one inch below the rim of the pot to allow for watering. Knock the pot on the table to settle the compost and leave the surface level.

Water at once, filling the space between the levels of the soil and the rim of the pot. Water when dry, increasing amount and frequency as the flowers and leaves emerge. A period of darkness is not necessary for these bulbs.

After flowering, cut off the flowers leaving the stalk to die down gradually. Cut stalk off just above the bulb when it has yellowed and shrivelled. Continue to water to keep the leaves growing because they feed the bulbs ready for flowering the following year. Bulbs that have leaves that completely die back should be dried off gradually when the leaves begin to yellow. *Hippeastrum, Vallota, Clivia* and *Nerine* all need a period of rest with little or no water and no feeding before being started into flower again.

SPECIFIC INSTRUCTIONS FOR INDIVIDUAL PLANTS

HIPPEASTRUM (AMARYLLIS)—THE BARBADOS LILY

This is a large lily-shaped flower, quite the queen of bulbs, in wonderful colours of pink, orange, flame, red, white, sometimes striped. The bulbs which can be up to 6 inches in diameter are relatively expensive but are a good investment for the beauty of the flowers and years of growth. Buy

Nerine

Hippeastrum

Vallota

a bulb at least 2½ inches in diameter with roots and perhaps top growth showing. Prepared bulbs are available for Christmas flowering.

PLANTING

Plant in February—April for late March—June flowering; October for Christmas.

Soak roots and the lower part of the bulb in tepid water for about five days. Plant in a pot which gives about an inch of space all round the bulb. *Hippeastrum* flowers better when pot-bound. Crocks must be used, as good drainage is essential. Use John Innes No. 2 or 3 compost and mound the compost into a cone placing the bulb on top with the roots spread out. About half the bulb should appear above the soil after planting. Water and place in a position where the bottom of the pot can be warm, such as on a shelf over a radiator, on a mantelpiece over a fire, on the top of of the television set, on a sunny windowsill or in the airing cupboard.

FURTHER CARE

Do not water for about two weeks, then water sparingly. Keep the temperature around 65—70°F and never below 60°F. Move to a sunny window when buds appear.

Water should always be tepid and directed on to the compost. The pot should never stand in water.

Feed weekly when growing well. When in full bloom move to a cooler place for longer flowering.

After flowering remove faded flower and stalk but leave main stem. Cut off main stem after it has yellowed, close to the bulb. Do not allow seeds to form which weakens the bulb. After flowering continue to water and feed and leave in the sun. Gradually reduce water from late August until end of September. Keep dry from end of September in a cool room for at least three months. Then start into the growth cycle again, by watering and placing in a warm spot.

Repot only every three to four years. An inch of soil may be replaced on the top each year.

CHRISTMAS FLOWERING

For Christmas flowering it is necessary to plant specially prepared bulbs in mid-October and to keep them in a temperature of not less than 65°F night and day.

NERINE (GUERNSEY LILY)

This plant bears rose-pink flowers in umbels from September to November, which appear before the leaves have grown well, from a spherical bulb with a long thin neck.

PLANTING

Plant in autumn in John Innes No. 2 compost. The flowers look better grouped three or four to a 6-inch pot. Cover half way up the neck with compost. Water and place in a sunny position.

FURTHER CARE

When the flower buds appear, probably in September, increase watering. Feed weekly when the foliage is well developed for about two months. Reduce water when the leaves begin to yellow until the next flower buds appear, as a rest is needed. The minimum winter temperature should be 50°F but the bulbs should stay in a sunny position.

Repot every four to five years in August but the top soil in the pot may be replaced annually. Offsets may be planted separately, when repotting, in John Innes No. 1 compost first and when they get bigger into John Innes No. 2. *Nerine* blooms better when pot-bound.

VALLOTA (SCARBOROUGH LILY)

Bright scarlet flowers bloom in clusters on stout stems with green strap-shaped leaves. The flowers look like a miniature *Hippeastrum*. Leaves and flowers appear together in August—September from large oval bulbs.

PLANTING

Plant two or three together in a large pot with the tips protruding above the John Innes No. 2 compost in June—July. A good watering is required after potting. Little heat is necessary and 50°F is warm enough. The pots should be placed in a sunny position.

FURTHER CARE

Increase water as the leaves appear and the flower opens, and begin to feed weekly. Reduce water and stop feeding after flowering. Remove flowers as they fade and stems when they become yellow. Stop watering between February and May.

Repot every three to four years as flowering is better when *Vallota* is pot-bound. When offsets fill the pot it is necessary to repot and they can be planted separately.

CLIVIA (KAFFIR LILY)

Orange, scarlet or yellow flowers clustered in umbels and dark green strap-shaped leaves.

PLANTING

Plant one to a pot in spring (5-inch pots) with John Innes No. 2 compost. Moderate heat (around 60°F) is sufficient—but it cannot stand frost.

FURTHER CARE

Clivia flowers in late spring but the foliage remains all year. Watering should be increased as the flower buds appear and weekly feeding should begin when the stem is about 6 inches long.

Remove faded flowers and stems as they yellow. A rest is essential and watering should be reduced and feeding should stop after mid-October. A little water in alternate weeks is sufficient, depending on the dryness of the room.

Pot on after flowering every two or three years until a 10-inch pot is reached. When this is full of roots, division becomes necessary. Shake away the old compost, remove any rotten sections of root, take off any young shoots, divide and replant. Flowering may be postponed a year after this as root disturbance causes a setback.

LACHENALIA (CAPE COWSLIP)

Small bell-shaped flowers in orange and yellow, sometimes pale blue, in late winter and spring, with strap-shaped leaves.

PLANTING

Pot in August and September in John Innes No. 2 compost, five to a 6-inch pot. Cover the bulbs with 1 inch of compost and keep in maximum light and at a minimum temperature of 45°F.

FURTHER CARE

Water sparingly at first, increasing when leaves appear. Reduce watering after flowering and keep the pots dry in July before repotting in August. Offsets should be repotted and will flower in one or two years.

FREESIA

Very fragrant, small flowers in beautiful and varied colours, grown from corms. The flowers, on erect stems, last a long time. Double-flowering varieties are especially lovely.

PLANTING

Plant from August to November, six to a 5-inch pot, with John Innes No. 2 compost. Just cover the tops with compost and then add a 1-inch layer of peat.

Lachenalia

Freesia

Clivia

Put into a cool place (minimum temperature 45°F) and give little water until growth begins. When there are seven leaves from a corm the pot can be put in a warmer position and the top peat removed. (Temperatures above 60°F are too warm.) Increase water and feed fortnightly once flower buds appear. Insert sticks to support the long flower stems. Flowering is from January to April. Reduce water after flowering and allow to dry completely and leave until early August. Take out of the pot and put the corms in a dry place removing offsets to plant separately. Freesias should be replanted each year.

OTHER FLOWERS FOR INDOORS
CONVALLARIA (LILY OF THE VALLEY)

This is not really a bulb but a fleshy crown. The fragrant white flowers grow like tiny bells on a short stem.

PLANTING
Plant in October and November, twelve to a 6-inch pot for a good display, in moist John Innes No. 2 compost. Wet the roots before planting and separate the roots as you plant. The tip of the crown should be above the compost. After potting keep moist by covering the tips with moist peat.

FURTHER CARE
Leave the pot in a heated room and a shady place until the new growth is 3—4 inches high. Then place in a warmer (about 65°F), light position and remove the peat. Always keep the pot moist.

After flowering discard the plants or plant out in the garden after gradually getting the plant used to cooler conditions. They need a slightly shady position.

LILIUM (LILY)
Beautiful, large fragrant flowers on long stems which are very successful in pots. *Lilium auratum, L. longiflorum, L. speciosum* and *L. regale* are all suitable.

PLANTING

Plant in autumn or winter singly in 6-inch pots or in threes in 10-inch pots, well crocked for good drainage, in John Innes No. 2 compost, covering with 1½ inches of compost. Leave room to add more soil.

FURTHER CARE

Keep in a cool, but frostproof place, preferably dark. Water sparingly. Bring gradually into light when the top growth is 3 inches high. Water sparingly. When roots appear, add peat on the top of the compost. Water well when in good growth and feed once a week. Keep out of direct sun but in an airy position. Tie the long stems to canes pushed into the compost. Cut off faded flowers but leave the stems.

Reduce watering after the flowers fade and when the leaves die down, keep the bulbs dry until they are repotted the following autumn. Repot lilies that are in small pots every year and those in larger pots or tubs every second or third year with topsoil replaced carefully in between repotting.

TUBEROUS BEGONIAS

There are many varieties of begonias, some of which grow from tubers. These make good flowering plants for the house, especially the double-flowered varieties. They have flowers in pink, yellow, orange, white and rose which are large and beautiful and last from June to September. The leaves are glossy green with reddish undersides.

PLANTING

In March place the tubers in a box of moist peat 3 inches deep. The hollow side of the tuber should be uppermost and placed just under the surface of the peat. Cover the box with a sheet of glass and place in a warm room about 65°F. When young shoots appear, remove the glass. When there are two or three leaves pot the tubers singly in John Innes No. 2 compost in 6-inch pots.

FURTHER CARE

Water well and feed when the first flower buds appear. Keep in full sun until mid-April with a temperature of about 65°F. Shade from the summer sun from May to October unless the plants are in an east-facing window. Tie the stems to short canes for support. When smaller 'female' flowers appear beside the larger male ones, they should be cut off.

Reduce the watering in October and stop feeding. The plant will die down. Store the tubers in a dry place with a temperature of not less than 40°F. Start the tubers into growth again in early spring.

Tuberous Begonia

Convallaria: Lily of the Valley

Arum lily

Lilium

ZANTEDESCHIA (ARUM LILY, CALLA LILY)

The white 'flower' is really a spathe—the flower is the erect yellow centre. There are white, yellow, green and peach-coloured varieties of spathe. The leaves are large and handsome.

PLANTING

Plant in a 6-inch pot during August and September, barely covering the roots with John Innes No. 2. Water moderately and leave in a cool place for a month.

FURTHER CARE

In October move the pot into a warmer place but water well as the plant likes a humid atmosphere. When roots show on the surface add more compost. Feed weekly at least, and give plenty of water once the leaves appear.

Decrease water and stop feeding after flowering and move to a cool place to rest until August or September when the bulb should be repotted in fresh compost.

PLANTING TENDER BULBS

Bulb	When to plant	In flower	No. to a pot	How to plant
Hippeastrum (Amaryllis)	February—April	Late March—June or 7–10 weeks after planting depending on the house temperature	One in a pot which gives 1-inch space around the bulb	$\frac{1}{3}$—$\frac{1}{2}$ of the bulb should be above the compost
Prepared bulbs	October	Christmas		
Clivia	April—May	February—March	One in a 5-inch pot	Tip should be above the compost
Freesia, (a corm)	August—November	January—February	Six to a 5-inch pot	Cover with a 1 inch compost
Lachenalia	August—September	Christmas on	Six to a 5-inch pot	Cover with 1 inch compost
Lily of the Valley (a crown)	October—November	Christmas	Twelve to a 6-inch pot	Just cover with compost
Nerine	Autumn—early winter	September—November	Four to a 6-inch pot	Cover with 1 inch compost the neck
Vallota	June—July	August—September	One in a 4–5-inch pot or three together in a wider pot	The tip should be above the compost
Zantedeschia Arum lily	August—September	Spring	One in a 6-inch pot	Barely cover roots with soil

PLANTS FOR CHILDREN

Children love to grow plants and the miracle of growth comes as an exciting discovery to most of them.

Many a life-long love of plants has developed from being taught the care of plants as a child. Children have many interests, however, and there is much in life to be explored and enjoyed, so it is better to encourage the growing of only one or two simple plants at first.

The greatest difficulty seems to be in establishing a pattern of care in a child — watering is often completely forgotten, for instance. If possible, therefore, children should be encouraged to water when parents water plants, or on set days such as Saturdays or after regular weekly events. The plant should be in an easily accessible position.

It is important that the plant be regarded as the child's possession and not just another plant in his or her room, looked after by the parents. This gives a greater sense of responsibility and more interest.

Buying the plant in the first place can be an exciting excursion for a child but discretion is essential in the choice. An exotic plant with coloured leaves (such as a croton) is a great temptation but the final selection should be gently directed towards an easier-to-grow plant. This will save possible disappointment, if the plant dies, which may result in a lack of any further interest. (If a plant does die it is wise to be quick with a replacement to maintain interest.)

Another consideration is to buy a plant that grows quickly, as children like immediate results and are impatient for signs of life.

It is important to take an interest in the plants grown by a child, to talk about their care and to remark when new shoots appear.

SUGGESTIONS

CHLOROPHYTUM COMOSUM (SPIDER PLANT)

The young plantlets are fun for a child and can be a lesson in propagation, as it is very easy to grow new plants.

SPRING BULBS

Those that are prepared for Christmas flowering are a good buy as they can be planted to make Christmas presents for giving to older relatives. Bulbs are also fascinating to watch as they develop. One bulb could be sacrificed and cut open so the child can see the embryo flower.

A hyacinth bulb can be grown in a special glass made for one hyacinth and the roots will be clearly visible. Crocus will grow on pebbles in a bowl of water.

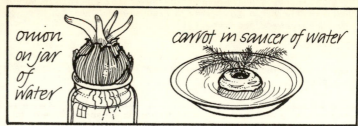

onion on jar of water

carrot in saucer of water

CARROTS AND ONIONS

A box of green groceries may contain a carrot or an onion with a tiny shoot. The onion may be put on to the neck of a jar of water and shoots will soon appear. A carrot should be sliced $\frac{1}{2}$ inch from the top and placed in a saucer of water. They will give interest for several weeks.

PIPS

Grapefruit and orange pips may be planted.

LILY OF THE VALLEY

A few pips of Lily of the Valley will give great pleasure as the flowers open.

BILLBERGIA

This plant is very easy and fast to grow and is no problem to divide. The flowers are exotic and interesting and it needs little water.

SAXIFRAGA SARMENTOSA

Another plant with 'babies' which is easily cared for and propagated.

GERANIUMS

These are easy and can be put into a sunny window. The flowers are gay and little watering is necessary.

A TERRARIUM

A terrarium could be made in an old goldfish tank or bowl. This would need no watering and could provide a lesson in the dependence of plants on a moist atmosphere.

GROUPED PLANTS

A group of small, easy-to-grow plants grown in one container has a good chance of survival.

CACTI AND SUCCULENTS

These are easy to care for and need little water but may not grow visibly enough for some children.

DISH GARDENS

Many children enjoy placing small accessories in a dish with growing plants to make a miniature garden, and some flower shows have a class for children's gardens.

SUCCULENTS AND CACTI

The word 'succulent' means full of juice, and with regard to plants it refers to any plants with thick, fleshy tissues which store water. They are members of widely varied plant families. Succulents originated in habitats where there are long periods of drought and they have adapted themselves so that they lose very little water through evaporation.

The skin or bark is often thick; they have simple shapes with a minimum surface area to save evaporation of water. Some store water in their stems and others in their leaves, which are thick and fleshy. The flowers vary according to the family to which the succulent belongs. *Echeveria* and Christmas cactus amongst many others are succulents that make excellent house plants.

Generally speaking, succulents need less water than other house plants and little in winter; soil that drains easily and quickly; some heat in winter; and plenty of sunshine.

CACTI

The chief characteristic of cacti is the areole, a growth like a tiny pin-cushion with woolly or bristly tufts. Flowers and new shoots usually appear at these points in spring. The flowers have no stalks.

Cacti are succulents and store water in their tissues to last them through droughts, as many originated in deserts. Most of them have no leaves but have stems adapted for storage which are either globular or cylindrical in shape. Some of these stems are strongly ribbed and others have tubercles, which are swollen parts usually arranged spirally around the plant. Other stems are flattened and may have spines that are sharp, bristly, barbed or hairy.

Cacti are useful for people with limited time as they need little attention. Many are small and suitable for limited spaces. They are excellent for hot, dry rooms and windows with direct summer sun where nothing else will grow.

Cacti look effective grouped together in a dish garden but they should not be combined with other house plants which do not like the same dry conditions.

CARE

Repot every other year in spring using five parts of John Innes No. 1 and one part coarse sand, or a compost sold especially for cacti, in a pot slightly larger than the previous one. Lift the cactus out of its pot by means of a band of folded newspaper held round the plant to avoid hurting the fingers.

Clean off dust with a soft brush.

Propagate by separating the offsets from the parent plant but dry these out for a few days before planting.

Place in the sun all the year round and keep the air dry.

In summer give plenty of water during the growing period, usually once a week unless the soil is moist. The water should drain through quickly as the roots do not like being in damp soil. Always pour away any surplus water. Regular feeding is unnecessary. In winter cacti can be in the sun but should be kept cool at a temperature of 40°–50°F and no warmer. This winter rest is necessary if flowers are to appear in the spring. No water is necessary in the winter if the cacti are kept cool.

EPIPHYLLUM

These are large-flowering cacti having flattened stems with wavy or notched edges. The flowers in May and June are bell-shaped and often brilliant, beautiful, and up to 6 inches across. Although they belong to the cacti family they originated in the tropical forests and not the desert. They are popular and easy to grow.

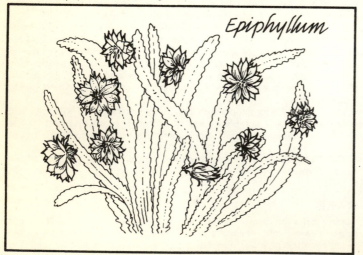

Epiphyllum

CARE

Full sun is not desirable — they thrive on an east-facing windowsill. A temperature of 60°F is desirable in summer and 50°F in winter. The roots should never be quite dry, even in winter.

Feed once every two weeks after the flower buds start to develop. Repot annually after flowering in John Innes No. 2 compost.

Propagate from 3-inch leaf sections taken at any time and inserted in sandy compost.

PART TWO— INDIVIDUAL PLANT CARE

The house plants included in this section are easy to grow. Some well-known plants, such as croton and *Aphelandra* have been omitted because they are more difficult.

The plants are listed alphabetically, and information is given in the following order: botanical name, popular name when there is one; a description of the plant: watering and spraying requirements; light and temperature requirements; feeding requirements; any special hints.

Aechmea rhodocyanea (Urn Plant)

A bromeliad (member of the pineapple family). An exotic plant with large, broad, strap-like leaves overlapping into a rosette which forms a water-tight central urn. It is as expensive to buy as it is slow to mature. Buy when the pink bract is a little above the water level in the urn. The bract may last for eight to ten months.

Keep urn filled with water but change it every few weeks to avoid stagnation. Little water is needed on the compost, which should be moist and never saturated.

Stands heat but not strong sunshine, 60°–65°F.

Feed sometimes through compost.

Do not clean leaves as this rubs away the natural 'bloom'. New growth forms at the base after flowering, when the mother plant dies off. The old plant may be cut away and the young ones left to grow on as a cluster.

Ananas (Pineapple)

This plant is a member of the bromeliad (or pineapple) family. The leaves may be grey or variegated cream and green in a rosette shape. They are sharp-edged so the plant needs space. A pineapple fruit may develop after three to four years in a greenhouse but this is unlikely in the house. The plant is often sold when bearing fruit.

Keep the compost moist but never saturated.

Needs a very light position and takes sun except on the hottest days. Temperature, between 55° and 70°F.

Feed sometimes through the compost.

Dies after producing a flower, but side shoots may be propagated.

Anthurium scherzerianum
(Flamingo Flower)

The easiest *Anthurium* to grow in the house. Tough, large green leaves, medium-size compact plant with exotic small red spathes which look like flowers. Long-lived.

Likes a moist atmosphere so spray and sponge. Keep compost moist; an outer pot of moist peat is helpful. Soft water is beneficial.

Shelter from strong sunlight; minimum temperature of 60°F.

Feed once a month except when without flower buds, when it should rest.

Repot when necessary with care using John Innes No. 2 compost and peat in equal quantities, as a rich soil is not suitable. Do not pack soil tightly around the roots.

Araucaria excelsa
(Norfolk Island Pine)

A green, coniferous 'tree' with needles on branches arranged in tiers around the main stem. A slow grower in the house or office but eventually very tall. Long-lived.

Keep moist as the soil dries out very quickly.

Good light, 45°–60°F but better on the cool side.

Feed in spring and summer.

Turn slightly now and again in spring and summer to keep a symmetrical growth. Once in a 6-inch pot, repot only every three years. May go in the garden in summer if shaded from strong sun.

Aspidistra lurida
(Cast Iron Plant)

Medium-sized plant with long, single, graceful leaves of dark green, sometimes striped with white. Very slow-growing and long-lived. A popular Victorian plant. May be neglected.

Should be kept on the dry side but will tolerate other conditions. Sponge leaves sometimes.

Avoid hot sun but otherwise grow in any light; flourishes in dim light. Suitable for shady corners. 55°F: can grow in unheated frost-free rooms.

Feed fortnightly.

Thrives in a smallish pot. Divide in spring when necessary. Buy the largest plant you can afford as growth is slow. It may be placed outside in summer in shade.

Aucuba japonica (Spotted Laurel)

Evergreen shrub, normally grown out of doors but very decorative indoors and useful for entrances and patios. Elegant, oval leaves in light green, spotted with yellow. Good feature plant. Large.

Water well in summer, and spray, as laurels will shed leaves if the air is too dry. Leaves may be sponged weekly.

Light position but tolerates shade; 45°–55°F.

Feed in spring and summer.

Trim and repot in spring. May be planted anywhere outside if not growing well indoors or if unattractive as an older plant.

Azalea indica

A popular flowering plant with small leaves and red, orange, pink, peach, white or mauve flowers. It should be bought when in bud with one or two flowers already open. If in tight bud the flowers may never open.

Plenty of water is essential as the plant will die if the compost is dry for long. Daily watering may be necessary to keep the compost wet. Rain water gives better results; soft water is better than hard as azaleas do not like lime. A plant may be watered by placing the pot in a bucket of water, removing it when the air bubbles stop rising.

Good light but not direct sunlight; 45°–55°F. Flowers last longer out of a warm room.

Feeding is not necessary.

Remove dead flowers. After flowering keep cool and moist then place outside after frosts are over. Put in a cool, light position in a hole filled with moist peat. See that the compost remains moist. Bring the plant indoors again in late September to a cool, light room. When potting on it is necessary to use a lime-free compost. Spraying helps to develop flower buds.

Begonia

There are many begonias. The tuberous ones are described on p. 60. Others are fibrous-rooted and rhizomatous. The leaves are very decorative and colourful.

Keep on the dry side but soil should be moist. Do not spray and avoid wetting leaves. Plunge into outer pots of moist peat for a necessary humid atmosphere or stand on a pebble tray.

Shady position, never bright sunlight; 55°–65°F. Never tolerates gas fumes. May suit artificial light.

Feed during growing season weekly.

The following are easy to grow:
- *B. rex*, with asymmetrical exotic leaves in many colours;
- *B. masoniana*, with a brown cross on the leaf;
- *B. heracleifolia*, very dark green star-shaped leaves;
- *B. maculata*, tall-growing, green leaves with small white spots;
- *B. metallica*, bronze-green leaves, tall-growing.

Begonia masoniana is illustrated left and B. rex right.

Beloperone (Shrimp Plant)

The flowering bracts look like large shrimps. Medium-sized plant. Small green leaves. The bracts are present most of the summer. Another variety has greenish-yellow bracts.

Water well during spring and summer.

Does well in an east-facing window with some sun; 50°–60°F.

Feeding should not be neglected—feed once a week.

Pot on at least once a year. Propagate from cuttings, placing more than one to a pot. Remove all the bracts as they appear for the first twelve months to make a strong plant. Pinch out in the early stages to make a bushy plant. Prune in spring. May lose leaves in winter.

Beloperone guttata is illustrated above.

Billbergia (Queen's Tears, Angel's Tears)

A member of the bromeliad (pineapple) family. Quick-growing. Rosette-shaped. Dark green, long, narrow leaves, very durable. Exotic flowering bracts droop down on long stems. Small to medium-sized.

Keep water in the vase-shaped centre, but a little is enough. Stands dry air.

Needs good light and can stand in the sun; 50°–60°F. Tolerates fumes.

No feeding necessary.

Divide often as it is a rapid grower and can easily become top heavy. A good plant to hang.

Camellia

Tough, glossy foliage with beautiful flowers in spring which may be double or single in white, pinks, reds or mauves. A shrub; hardy in the garden.

Water with soft, tepid water. Spray often, as a moist atmosphere is beneficial, especially when buds are large. Keep compost moist, never dry.

Dislikes fluctuating temperatures. Best in an east-facing window. Can stand sunshine. Winter: 40°–50°F; summer: 55°–60°F but stands warmer temperatures if in moist air.

Feed weekly but not just before or just after flowering.

Minimal pruning in spring only to keep the shape. Lime-free soil is essential. Constant change of position is harmful and it should be left in peace.

Campanula isophylla (Star of Bethlehem, Italian Bellflower)

Trailing plant which flowers profusely all though the summer with star-shaped blue, mauve or white flowers. Good for hanging up. Suitable for many conditions. Buy in bud.

Water very well, every day, when growing actively. Drying out causes shrivelling of the leaves. Keep fairly dry in winter.

Tolerates fluctuating temperatures if well watered and fed regularly. Minimum 40°F; airy, well-lit. Protect a little from strong summer sun.

Feed weekly in summer.

Remove dead flowers to prevent seeding which weakens the plant. Prune the stems right back after flowering to the top of the pot and place in a frost-free room which is cool. Repot in early spring. Young shoots easily root.

Chlorophytum comosum (Spider Plant)

Long, narrow, green and white leaves which grow with arching habit. Long runners on which new plantlets form.

Water freely in spring and summer, keeping soil moist.

Light position but grows with little light. Avoid direct sunlight; 55°–75°F, minimum 45°F (best around 55°F). Tolerates fumes.

Feed weekly in spring and summer.

Easy plant to grow and propagate. Good hanging plant as the plantlets can fall down gracefully. Better featured alone rather than mixed with other plants. Brown-tipped leaves appear unless potted on regularly, but these leaves may be cut off.

Chrysanthemum

Well-known flowering plant with many varieties throughout the year. Buy in bud for flowers which will last eight to ten weeks. Many colours and several flower forms including pompom, decorative, in-curved. Treated by the grower so that the height is restricted for a pot plant.

Water regularly and do not allow soil to dry out. Reduce water a little as the flowers open to prolong their life.

Light position; 55°–65°F; avoid direct sunlight.

Feeding unnecessary.

Discard after flowering or plant outside after gradually acclimatizing.

Cineraria

Large-leaved plant with attractive, clustered single or double flowers in blue, violet, purple, red or crimson, often with white. Should be bought in bud in winter or spring.

Water well. Do not spray.

Light but no direct sun; minimum temperature of 45°F. The flowers will fade quickly in a hot room. Avoid draughts.

Feed weekly when in flower.

Discard after flowering.

Cissus antarctica (Kangaroo Vine)

Natural climber with own tendrils. Heart-shaped, serrated, dark green, shiny leaves. May grow six to eight feet high. Grows quickly and soon covers a support, trellis or wall.

Water well in spring and summer, less in winter. Spray, as a moist atmosphere is desirable—otherwise leaves may drop off. Tolerates fumes.

Light but no direct sun. Very hardy and stands wide fluctuations in temperature: winter 50°F; summer 65°F.

Feed once a fortnight in spring and summer.

May be pruned in spring. Pot on every other year up to a 10-inch pot. Provide support such as trellis, wall, stake.

Coleus

Nettle-shaped leaves in various lovely colours, usually variegated. Small to medium size. Good mixed with other plants in bowls.

Water frequently in summer, less in winter.

Light position, takes summer sun, temperature about 60°F.

Feed weekly in summer.

Remove the unattractive flowers when they appear, to strengthen the leaves. Pinch out to keep bushy. Potting on may be necessary more than once during the summer. Usually thrown out when plant becomes leggy; new plants are easily rooted.

Cryptanthus (Earth Stars, Starfish Plant, Star Plant)

A compact, slow-growing, adaptable plant with hard, sharp leaves in a rosette shape and strikingly coloured. A member of the bromeliad (pineapple) family. There are several varieties. Useful for a bottle garden. Durable foliage.

Tepid water should be used. Avoid over-watering but keep soil moist in summer. Water sparingly in winter. Spray with tepid water. Good drainage is essential to avoid rotting. (There is no 'vase' to fill as with other bromeliads.)

Good light but no direct sun. Minimum 60°F.
Very weak feed once a fortnight.

New plants are propagated from small offsets at the base.

Cryptanthus tricolor is illustrated above and C. zonalus below.

Cyclamen

Well-known winter-flowering plant with heart-shaped leaves which are very attractive and often variegated. The flowers may be white, pink, red or mauve. It is better to buy the plant in bud in the autumn. It is not difficult to keep if properly treated but is unsuited to hot, dry rooms.

Water well and then allow the compost to dry out before watering again. Use tepid water, as cold may harm the roots. The plant should not stand in water so any surplus must be poured away. Avoid excessive wetness or dryness and water the soil, not the plant.

Very light position and sunshine from mid-October to mid-March. No strong sun in summer. 50°–55°F; airy; never place in a hot room.

Feed weekly but rest after flowering with less water and no food.

Normally discarded after flowering, otherwise repot in May, plunge into the garden in light shade and move indoors when flower buds appear. Plants are not usually as good as new ones. Dead flowers and leaves should be pulled off completely leaving no pieces, which will rot.

The Silver-leaf cyclamen is illustrated above.

Echeveria

A succulent with thick, juicy leaves in a rosette shape. A long stalk of small flowers sometimes appears. There are many varieties, mostly low-growing, in colours of pale green, blue-grey and bronze. Good in shallow bowls as the roots are short. Neglectable.
Very little water at any time, especially in winter. Keep water away from leaves to avoid spotting. No spraying.

Best in full sunlight which gives better colouring. Winter, 40°–50°F; summer, 55°–60°F.

Feed once a month in summer.

Grows out of doors in summer but should be brought in for the winter. When leggy cut the stem just above soil level where new growth will form. Pot the cut-off rosette. Repot annually in spring.

Fatshedera lizei (Climbing Fig-leaf Palm, Fat-headed Lizzie)

A cross between *Fatsia* and *Hedera* (ivy). It has five-lobed, bright green leaves on an upright stem. There is also a variegated variety. Medium size but may grow 8 feet tall. Leaves are larger than ivy but smaller than *Fatsia*.

Water well, keeping soil moist in summer, less so in winter. Spray and sponge leaves sometimes.

Light position, no direct sun, tolerant of shady situations. Minimum temperature 50°F; can get used to higher temperatures. Survives out of doors in milder, sheltered gardens as it is a hardy plant.

Feed fortnightly.

Support the tall stem. For a bushier plant pinch out the top in spring or summer. Repot annually in March. Cuttings root easily.

Fatsia japonica (Aralia)

Also called *Aralia sieboldii*. Quick-growing plant with shiny, large, leathery leaves having seven to nine lobes. There is a variegated variety. This is a plant that may be featured. It can grow very wide and requires space. Suitable for modern rooms. Good for patios; the all-green variety will grow permanently outside if sheltered from the wind and gradually acclimatized. Popular and very decorative.

Water well in summer, less well in winter. Spray sometimes and wash leaves.

Light position but tolerant of some shade. 45°–65°F. If in a hot room it may lose leaves, which yellow first.
Feed weekly in summer.

Hardy enough for cool entrance halls. The variegated *Fatsia* needs more warmth.

Aralia sieboldii is illustrated above.

Ferns

There are many species of fern, which are foliage plants. They vary greatly in form, size and habit and are excellent combined with other plants in bowls, often as a pleasing contrast to plainer leaf shapes.

A moist atmosphere is essential. Water well in summer, less well in winter. Do not allow the compost to dry out; good drainage is needed to prevent sogginess around the roots. Spray often. Small ferns are good in bottle gardens.

Shady positions but not dark corners; no direct sun. 45°F minimum temperature and cooler rooms. May be grown in artificial light.

Feed in summer monthly.

Repot carefully as the roots are sensitive.

Good varieties for the house are *Asparagus sprengeri Adiantum* (Maidenhair Fern) bottom left; Polystichums, bottom right; Pteris, top right; and *Nephrolepis*, top left. All are very adaptable and easy to grow.

Ficus benjamina

This is the weeping fig which may eventually grow into a small tree but is slow-growing. Graceful. Buy a large plant if possible.

Water well in summer, keep just moist in winter. Sponge and spray.

Well-lit position out of direct sunshine; 60°–72°F.

Feed every two weeks.

May drop yellowed leaves when first in the home but given the correct conditions it will settle down.

Ficus elastica robusta (Rubber Plant)

A very popular house and office plant which can be featured. It is suitable for modern rooms. Large oval green leaves; there is also an attractive variety with variegated leaves, which is slower-growing.

Water well in spring and summer, less well in winter, using tepid water. Over-watering in winter can cause the leaves to fall off. Compost should dry out between waterings. Sponging of leaves using tepid water is essential now and again to remove dust.

Will grow in poor light; 50°–60°F. The variegated type needs a little more warmth. Feed weekly in spring and summer.

May stay several years in the same pot once it has reached the 10-inch size. A rubber plant may grow very tall (ceiling high) but can be reduced through air-layering and made into more than one plant.

Ficus pumila (Creeping Fig)

Long-lasting plant which may be grown as a trailer or climber. Good for hanging up. Small leaves; good to mix with other plants in bowls.

Keep moist; a humid atmosphere is necessary, so spray, using tepid water.

Plenty of light, and sunshine except in mid-summer; 60°–72°F.

Feed weekly in summer.

Pinch out sometimes to improve the appearance. Should be potted on if supplied in a small pot. Can be pruned when overgrown.

Fuchsia (Lady's Eardrop)

A plant with pendulous, bell-shaped, pink, red, white or violet flowers, often with white, or mixed in colour. They may be double or single. A good hanging plant.

Needs large quantities of water in summer or it suddenly wilts. Much less water is needed from October until spring. Spray leaves sometimes. Never allow to dry out completely.

Very light, airy position, but no direct sunlight; 40°–65°F.

Feed weekly in summer.

Remove dead flowers. Remove seedpods or flowering will stop. Discard after flowering or place in a cool, frost-free place after cutting down. Repot in spring, pinching out for a bushy plant as it grows.

Gloxinia (Sinningia)

Trumpet-shaped flowers in brilliant blues, violets, reds, sometimes with white with a velvety texture. It should be bought when in bud.

Use tepid water on the compost and not on the flowers or leaves. Spray when not in flower. Keep moist.

Light position but not direct sunlight; 55°–65°F.

Feed weekly during flowering season.

After flowering allow to die down and do not feed. Reduce water gradually. Remove dead flowers and leaves and store the tuber in a dry place, such as a cupboard, for the winter in a temperature of about 55°F. Discard three-year-old tubers. Place the others in moist peat and when new growth is 2 inches high repot in 5-inch pots of John Innes No. 2 compost, placing the top of the tuber level with the compost surface. The temperature should be 70°F. If not to be grown next year, discard.

Grevillea robusta
(Silk Oak, Australian Wattle)

Bronze-green, fern-like leaves which are silky on the underside. Upright growth, fast-growing, medium to tall.

Water well in spring and summer, less in winter. Likes a dry atmosphere.

Very hardy, thriving in cool, airy positions. Light position but not direct sun; 50°–65°F.

Feed fortnightly using a weak solution in spring and summer for a tall plant.

Repot every other year — annually if necessary.

Gynura

Purple-tinted leaves which are very ornamental. A trailer. Needs replacing regularly.

Keep soil moist and spray with tepid water.

Any reasonable light but no direct sun; 50°–60°F. An east-facing window is best.

Feed weekly.

Remove the flowers, which smell unpleasant. Throw away, after taking cuttings, when the plant becomes leggy or leaves become green. Young plants are a better purple in colour and more attractive.

Gynura sarmentosa is illustrated above.

Hedera (Ivy)

There are many varieites of ivy, which is a tough climber, a trailer or a bushy plant with several decorative uses. May have plain green leaves or variegated ones with grey, silver, cream or yellow. Varies in size from small to medium. Similar conditions are necessary for all ivies. Good in bowls or troughs with other plants.

Give little water in winter. Keep moist in spring and summer but never over-water. Spraying the leaves is essential especially in a dry atmosphere.

Any light. May be grown in sun if atmosphere is kept moist. Tolerates some shade; 45°–60°F but prefers the cooler temperatures. Very hardy, tolerant of fumes but dislikes hot, dry rooms.

Feed once a month in summer.

Needs support as a climber. Remove growing tips for a bushy plant. Good hanging plant. Cut off stems that are too long or wind back around the **plant and pin down**. Repot every second year in spring. If the leaves turn brown, plant outside. Easily rooted cuttings.

Hedera canariensis is illustrated above.

Heptapleurum arboricola

Dainty, umbrella-shaped green leaves on branches around a central stem. Branches well if growing tip is removed. Good medium-sized plant for featuring.

Moderate water in spring and summer, less in winter.

Good light, no direct sun in summer; 50°–65°F, cooler temperature preferred.

Feed weekly in summer.

Turn the plant sometimes as the leaves turn towards the light. Needs support if grown tall. Top can be pinched out if it becomes too tall.

Hibiscus (Rose of China)

Large, red, pink, orange or lemon flowers which normally last only a day but flowers are plentiful on established plants. Double or single blooms.

Keep soil moist and provide a humid atmosphere by spraying often. Water a little in winter, or dry out and keep warm and start watering into growth again in spring.

Light position and can take some summer sunlight. An even temperature is important or flower buds may drop off. 55°–65°F.

A greedy feeder, so feed often.

Shorten stems and repot in spring when necessary.

Hoya (Wax Plant)

A climber with smeet-smelling waxy white flowers and small, fleshy, green leaves. A variegated variety has peach-coloured leaves when young.

Keep moist in summer, dryish in winter. Never over-water. Spraying is beneficial.

Needs good light, 55°–65°F. Protect from direct summer sun – east window best.

Feed weekly when new growth starts in spring. Stop feeding when buds form.

Needs trellis or wires for support. Do not move frequently and preferably keep always in the same position. *Hoya* does not like stopping or pruning but when becoming overgrown it can be pruned after flowering. Leave dead flowers on the plant as new flower buds will form.

Hydrangea

Medium to large plant with big white, pink, red, blue or mauve flowers, sometimes multi-coloured, in spring and summer.

Never allow to dry out – watering may be needed daily – and good drainage is necessary.

Light position but not direct sun. Cool room, 50°–60°F.

Feed once a week before and during flowering.

After flowering discard or cut down to 1 inch above the old growth (brown wood) and plant in the garden, watering well at first.

Impatiens (Busy Lizzie, Balsam)

A small, homely, fast-growing plant with red, orange, white or pink flowers that bloom nearly all year. Leaves may be green or bronze. Compact, low-growing, unless potted on.

Water very well in summer, less in winter, spray sometimes. Never allow to dry out.

Light position essential. Cool room, minimum temperature 50°F.

Feed weekly in spring and summer.

Cut back in spring to induce new growth but rarely keep for longer than eighteen months as it becomes leggy. Non-flowering shoots are easily propagated at any time.

Impatiens petersiana is illustrated above.

Ipomoea (Morning Glory)

An annual and a climber with blue flowers throughout the summer. Will grow out of doors but does better indoors. There is also a perennial variety for the house.

Needs a lot of water in summer when well grown. Spray leaves.

Needs sunshine. 50°–60°F.

Feed weekly with diluted solution.

Provide support for the stems. Cut back when overgrown. Do not repot. Sow seeds in early spring, one seed to a big pot, $\frac{1}{2}$ inch under the surface. Keep in a warm room (see section on seed-sowing, pp. 48–9).

Jasminum polyanthum (Jasmine)

Not an especially attractive plant in appearance but the white flowers are very fragrant. Small leaves and many small flowers. Trellis should be provided for larger plants as it is a climber.

Keep soil moist and spray often.

Stands sun except direct summer sun. Needs full light. Winter, 45°F, summer, 55°–65°F.

Feed once a fortnight in spring and summer.

Pot on after flowering. Grows quickly and may need pruning, which does not harm the plant. Growth stops in winter and leaves may be shed but growth starts again in spring.

Kentia

More correctly *Howea*, this is an elegant palm which is very decorative and may be featured or combined with other plants in a trough or bowl. Traditional or modern rooms are suitable. Long-lived and durable, slow to mature, expensive.

Water well in summer and keep the soil moist in winter. A moist atmosphere is essential so spray and sponge sometimes to remove dust. Can be placed in an outer pot of moist peat or combined with other plants which provide a moist atmosphere.

Light preferable but tolerant of shade. No strong sun. 60°–70°F.

Feed fortnightly in spring and summer.

Repot only when pot-bound, being careful not to damage the sensitive roots. Avoid draughts which can brown the leaves. Also, leaves do not like to be continually brushed against.

Kalanchoë

A small, succulent plant with fleshy leaves. The small red flowers may appear throughout the winter.

Water fairly well in winter growing period but never over-water as this will cause the stems to rot.

Light, sunny position, 50°–65°F.

Feed fortnightly.

Remove dead flowers and stalks at once. Cut back after flowering and repot. There will soon be sufficient shoots to take cuttings. May go outside in the sun in mid-May.

Laurus nobilis (Bay Tree)

A hardy, evergreen shrub useful for entrances and patios. It is grown as standard (a mop-head on a tall step) or in a cone shape. Expensive but decorative.

Water well in summer, less in winter.

Good light and full winter sun. Protect from frost, otherwise stands low temperatures.

Feed weekly in summer.

Protect from cold winds if outside. Can be trimmed to keep a good shape.

Maranta

Several varieties, the most common being *Maranta leuconeura kerchoveana* which has pale green oval leaves with dark brown blotches. *M. l. erythrophylla* is a darker green with fascinating markings in red-brown. Good in bowls with other plants.

Keep soil moist and spray, as a moist atmosphere is desirable. Put with other plants or sink the pot into an outer pot containing moist peat. Dead tips mean too dry an atmosphere. Feed once a week in summer. Easily divided, does well in a shallow pot.

No direct sunlight, tolerates shade, 55°–65°F.

Maranta kerchoveana is illustrated in inset. M. erythrophylla is the main photo.

Monstera deliciosa (Swiss Cheese Plant)

Large, dramatic, deeply cut and perforated mid-green leaves. This big plant needs space and can grow very tall and/or wide. Good plant for featuring in modern rooms. Can be a climber or a bushy spreader. Aerial roots hang down from the stem and should not be removed. Tough, long-lived, very popular.

Water well in summer, less in winter. Sponge the leaves and spray sometimes. Do not handle young unfolding leaves.

Medium to poor light, no direct sun, 55°–65°F.

Feed fortnightly in spring and summer.

Tie aerial roots together if necessary. Tuck the ends in the compost or under the pot when in a decorative outer pot. If a climber is desired, provide support or tie up. For a bushy plant cut off the top. Repot every two or three years.

Neanthe bella (Parlour Palm)

The correct botanical name is actually *Chamaedorea elegans*. This is a compact palm which does not grow high. Long, green leaves. It can live for many years. A good plant for a bottle garden. Slow growing.

Needs plenty of tepid water in summer, and spraying with tepid water, but wet combined with cold air gives brown leaf tips. Give less water in winter.

Light position, 55°–65°F; sun or shade is tolerated.

Feed once a fortnight in summer.

Pot on only once in three years being careful not to damage the roots. Keep away from draughts and in a position where it is not touched by people brushing against it.

Passiflora caerulea
(Passion Flower, Maypop)

Fascinatingly beautiful flowers and a rapid growing climber. The flowers only last about two days but are worth it and there is usually at least one flower every day. Can become rampant.

Water well in summer.

Keep frost free; can go outside all summer — it is hardy in sheltered conditions.

Feed weekly in summer; but will grow without feeding.

Prune drastically in spring. Flowers well if the roots are restricted, that is in a small pot. Trellis necessary.

Pelargonium

Pelargonium zonale is called geranium; *P. peltatum* is a trailing plant, which is excellent in bowls and hung up. Regal pelargoniums, also known as *P. domesticum*, are usually blotched or veined with darker shades. The geranium is very popular and cheerful, and can stand neglect. Flowers are white, pink, salmon, red, orange or purple. There are many varieties.

Water well in summer but allow to dry between waterings. The drainage should be good. Keep much drier in winter.

Sunny posititition or full light. Minimum, 45°–50°F; 60°–70°F is ideal. Feed older plants once a fortnight in summer.

Remove dead flowers and leaves. Plants may be kept for several years but flowering is not as satisfactory. Cut back after flowering and keep in a frost-free room in winter. Repot in March. Pinch back often to encourage bushiness until flower buds appear. Cuttings may be taken in August for new plants. If winter flowers are desired, remove flower buds as they appear until late August.

P. zonale is illustrated.

Peperomia

Slow-growing, small, bushy and compact plant with several varieties. Small, very ornamental leaves sometimes fleshy and variegated, in greens. Good in bowls of mixed plants. Some varieties have long, thin flowering spikes.

Keep soil moist but not wet and allow to dry out between waterings. Keep drier in winter. Spray sometimes, as a moist atmosphere is more important than wet compost. Will survive if left dry for a while.

Light position out of strong sunlight. Minimum temperature, 55°F.

Little feeding is necessary.

Seldom needs repotting and the small roots are better grown in a small pot. Prefers a soilless compost and crocks in as much as one-third of the pot.

Top illustration is Peperomia hederaefolia and the bottom one is Peperomia magnoliaefolia.

Philodendron bipinnatifidum

A large plant which needs space but excellent as a decorative feature plant. Large, deeply cut, green, almost triangular leaves radiating from the centre on long stems. Good on a pedestal or large table. Good for modern rooms and long-lived.

Keep moist, neither dry nor over-watered. Needs a moist atmosphere so may be planted in an outer pot of moist peat.

Light or semi-shade but not direct sunlight or leaves turn yellow, 55°–65°F with higher temperatures preferable. Avoid fluctuating temperatures and draughts.

Feed weekly in spring and summer.

Any aerial roots that grow should be placed into the moist peat surrounding the pot or into the compost.

Philodendron scandens (Sweetheart Plant)

There are many varieties of *Philodendron* but this is the easiest to grow and most popular. Medium-sized climber or bushy plant with small, green, heart-shaped leaves. A tough, neglectable plant.

Water well in summer, less in winter; spray sometimes. Also known as the bathroom plant, as it grows well in a warm steamy atmosphere. Keep moist for best results.

Likes light but good in darker places and will grow under electric light that is on for twelve hours out of twenty-four. Keep out of direct sun; 50°–65°F, but prefers the higher temperature. Tolerates gas fumes.

Feed fortnightly in spring and summer.

Remove weak winter growth to a good leaf in spring. Pinch out tip for a bushy plant. Support for a climber. Repot every other year in spring. Trailers may be pinned down on the compost for new plants.

Philodendron scandens is illustrated above.

Pilea (Aluminium Plant)

Small, compact plant with leaves that may be plain green or attractively marked. *P.* Moon Valley is an easy variety to grow.

Keep the soil moist in the pot and spray often, as a damp atmosphere is helpful. Use deep-dish method sometimes. Tepid water.

Moderate light and no summer sun but winter sun is acceptable; 55°–65°F.

Feed weekly when growing well.

Prune well in spring and repot if necessary. Does not last well as an attractive plant so is best renewed from cuttings every year or so. Remove tips of new plants to encourage bushiness.

Bottom illustration is Pilea cadierei nana. The top illustration is Pilea 'Moon Valley'.

Plumbago

A climber with pale blue, cascading flowers rather like a small phlox. There is also a white variety.

Water well in summer, very little in winter. Spray well as humid conditions are beneficial.

Can stand full sunlight, otherwise a very light position 45°–55°F in winter, 55°–65°F in summer.

After flowering prune shoots to 2–3 inches from the base. Repot in spring if necessary. Needs a very large pot and trellis or canes for support.

Poinsettia (Christmas Flower)

This is *Euphorbia pulcherrima* with red, pink or white bracts, which look like flowers, appearing around Christmas.

Little water; allow to dry out between waterings or the leaves yellow and drop off. Tepid, not cold, water.

Light sunny position, 60°–65°F, away from radiators.

Feeding not necessary when bracts are present.

Usually disposed of after the bracts drop off as flowering bracts are difficult to produce a second year.

Primula

Popular plants in the spring with primrose-shaped flowers. Long flowering period. Small. Varieties normally available are *P. obconica* with large flowers, *P. malacoides*, *P. sinensis* and *P. acaulis*.

Water well when growing, keeping the soil moist and not allowing it to dry out. Do not spray when in flower.

A light position but not direct sunlight; 50°–55°F.
Feed regularly to have a succession of flowers.

Remove dead flowers. Discard after flowering. *P. acaulis* may be planted outside.

P. acaulis is illustrated above; P. obconica below.

Rhoicissus rhomboidea (Grape Ivy)

Dark green, shiny, toothed leaves; a climber or trailer which grows rapidly and branches freely. Leaflets grow from the stem in groups of three from one point. Probably the toughest of all house plants; stands gas fumes and dry air.

Plenty of water in spring and summer, keeps just moist in winter. A humid atmosphere is desirable so frequent spraying is helpful but withstands dry air better than most vines.

Good light but never strong sunshine. Satisfactory in shade or in a dark position with the help of artificial lighting. Good in central heating. Summer temperature 55°–65°F; winter 45°–55°F.

Feed fortnightly in spring and summer.

Pinch out growing tips for a bushy plant; otherwise tie to a wall or support with a trellis, sticks or netting for a climber. Also good as a hanging plant. Repot annually in April. Prune when necessary using the cuttings to propagate new plants.

Saintpaulia (African Violet)

Small, attractive plant with pink, blue, mauve or white flowers which may be single, double or ruffled. Silky grey-green leaves. May flower almost all year with the right treatment.

Water well in summer by placing the pot on a saucer of water until the compost is moist. This avoids wetting leaves and flowers. Use tepid water as cold water is harmful. Water when leaves seem slightly limp to the touch. Moist air is beneficial so standing on a pebble tray or in a pot of damp peat is good.

Very light or sunny position but not direct summer sun. Prefers fourteen hours of light in every twenty-four, which can be electric light. 60°–70°F, even temperature not fluctuating.

Feed in spring and summer with a weak solution fortnightly using a fertilizer with high phosphate content.

Remove any dead flowers and leaves at once. Pot on about every second year in shallow pots that seem on the small side. Dust foliage sometimes with a soft brush.

Sansevieria trifasciata Laurentii (Mother-in-law's Tongue)

A decorative, erect plant of medium to large size which thrives on neglect. The rigid, long, fleshy leaves 2–3 inches wide are edged with yellow and striped with darker green. The barb at the tip is the reason for the popular name. Slow-growing.

Needs very little water and can go for months without. The compost should be built up to the rim of the pot to avoid over-watering. It should not sink down in the centre around the plant or water will collect. A dribble once in two weeks in summer and once a month in winter is sufficient. Not good mixed with other plants in a bowl because most of them need more water. It could have the roots wrapped in polythene to prevent water reaching them in mixed plant bowls, but is better grown alone.

Good in full sun but shade is acceptable. Can take high or low temperatures but prefers high. Minimum 50°F. Tolerates fumes. Cold and wet conditions are usually fatal.

Feeding unimportant but can be fed once a month in summer.

Rarely needs repotting. A clay pot is better as the plant can be top-heavy. Divide the roots when pot bound.

Saxifraga sarmentosa
(Mother of Thousands)

Small plant with rapid growth. Dark green, round, marbled and hairy leaves with coloured veins, underside purple-red. It belongs to the strawberry family and new plants grow at the end of runners. Attractive as a hanging plant so that the plantlets droop freely. Grows well in most places.

Water well in summer; less in winter. Keep moist.

Light sunless position. Suitable for unheated, frost-free rooms. 50°–60°F.

Feed once a fortnight in spring and summer.

New plants can be produced by pegging down plantlets.

Schefflera

Green leaves like rays of the sun divided into a number of leaflets. More decorative as a mature plant and good featured alone. Medium to large in size. Slow grower. Leaves are green and glossy.

Water and spray often, especially in a warm room.

Tolerates sun other than in mid-summer, 55°–65°F. Light, airy conditions.

Feed once a week.

A wide pot is necessary.

Schlumbergera
(Christmas Cactus, Crab Cactus)

Formerly known as *Zygocactus truncatus*. A pendulous, spreading plant with long segmented stems that look more like leaves. May be grown as a hanging plant with success. Cerise flowers appear near Christmas time at the end of the stems. Medium size, normally long-lived. One of the easiest plants to grow.

Keep the compost moist but give a little water in October while flower buds are forming. Increase water as buds are seen. Allow to rest again with little water after the flowers drop off. Never saturate.

Light window out of direct sun; 55°–65°F.

Feed fortnightly but not during October or for six weeks after flowering.

Keep the plant in exactly the same position when the buds are about to open, otherwise the buds may be shed. Fluctuating temperatures may also cause shedding of buds. Cuttings may be taken at any time.

Sempervivum
(Houseleek, Hen and Chickens)

A succulent plant with fleshy leaves in rosettes. Almost hardy in the garden. Neglectable plant. Many varieties.

Little water at any time and almost none in winter.

Full sunshine or good light.

The coolest place in the house, so long as it is frost-free.

Feeding not necessary.

Use shallow pots for the short roots. Small plants at the side of the stem can be pulled off and planted separately.

Senecio macroglossus
(German Ivy, Cape Ivy)

Quick-growing, small-leafed plant with almost triangular, rather fleshy, cream-variegated leaves. A climber which needs support. It looks like an ivy, for which it is often mistaken.

Moderate watering in summer. No spraying.

Well-lit position; tolerates dry atmosphere but not oil or gas fumes; 55°–65°F.

Feed once a fortnight.

Cuttings are easily rooted. The tips should be removed when the young plants start growing to make them bushier. The natural waxy coating on the leaves should not be removed.

Solanum capsicastrum
(Winter Cherry)

Small green leaves and large orange or red berries in autumn and winter which stay on the plant for months. Usually purchased when berried and later discarded.

Keep the compost moist and do not allow to dry out. Waterlogging is also bad for the plant.

Needs a very light, sunny position and deteriorates quickly in poor light; 55°–65°F. Berries last longer at the lower temperature. No gas fumes.

Feed weekly.

After the berries drop in spring, it may be repotted and kept in a cool room with good light, but the plant is usually discarded. Cuttings may be taken, and it may be grown from seed. Pinch out tips for a bushy plant.

Stephanotis floribunda (Madagascar Jasmine)

A twining shrub with small, very fragrant waxy, white flowers which grow in clusters, often used in wedding bouquets. Support is needed and the stems may be wound around an oval wire back and forth. Expensive to buy but long-lasting.

Use tepid water as cold is harmful. Do not saturate but keep the soil moist in summer, very dry in winter. Likes very moist air so an outer moist peat pot is helpful. Good drainage necessary.

Good light but not direct summer sunshine. Winter 50°–55°F; summer 60°–70°F. Better in an even temperature than in one that fluctuates. Stands plenty of winter sunlight.

Feed weekly in summer.

Remove dead shoots in spring.

Zebrina pendula

A good, small plant for hanging up. Dark green and brown leaves with the underside purple. Good for mixing with other plants in bowls and troughs. Quick-growing trailer.

Keep moist.

Light position, 50°–60°F. The variegation may fade in shade.

Feed once a fortnight in summer.

Remove any plain green growth as it appears. Take cuttings when growth becomes straggly to start new plants, placing five cuttings in a $3\frac{1}{2}$-inch pot.

Tradescantia (Wandering Sailor) A tough, easy to grow, small plant in green, purple, gold, pink, silver, according to variety, should be treated similarly. *Tradescantia is illustrated above; Zebrina below.*